The Way He Walked

A 21-DAY JOURNEY TO LIFE AS IT SHOULD BE

DR SEAN NOLAN ThD

Ark House Press
arkhousepress.com
Design by initiateagency.com

Cataloguing in Publication Data:
Title: The Way He Walked | ISBN: 978-1-7643820-7-6 (pbk)
Subjects: REL006700 RELIGION / Biblical Studies / Bible Study Guides; REL074000 RELIGION / Christian Ministry / Pastoral Resources; REL012120 RELIGION / Christian Living / Spiritual Growth.
Edited by Mrs Julia Hosking and Dr Robert Doyle PhD.

FOREWORD

by Evangelist Will Graham

I first had the blessing of ministering alongside Sean Nolan in the small Australian outback mining town of Broken Hill (an event you'll read about on Day 18 in this book). We saw God do many amazing things during our brief time in that beautiful and historic community, but one particular story sticks in my mind.

A young lady named Denise arrived in Broken Hill in the dark of night. She managed a few fitful hours of sleep in the bus station, with plans to set off by foot the next morning. Her goal was to hitchhike 500 kilometers across treacherous terrain to Adelaide. She'd even made a large hand-written cardboard sign reading "ADELAIDE" to use in flagging down potential rides.

We had just finished up *Reality Australia* (as our evangelistic outreach was called) and were gathered in a local Broken Hill coffee shop rejoicing at what God had done. I didn't even realize it at the time, but—before leaving town—Denise entered the coffee shop to see what all of the commotion was about.

A lady named Margaret—the wife of the local leader who served as the chairperson of *Reality Australia*—began a conversation with Denise. Filled with confidence and joy from witnessing so many friends and neighbors respond to the Gospel over the previous few days, Margaret boldly asked Denise, "Can I tell you about Jesus?"

At the name of Jesus, Denise began to cry. Margaret gently began sharing the Gospel with the young lady, and soon prayed with Denise as she surrendered her eternity into the hands of the Savior.

You can imagine the celebration in that coffee shop! We were already excited by the response to the Gospel at *Reality Australia*, but God wasn't done. He had brought us one more!

But that wasn't all…

Learning of Denise's plan to hitchhike to Adelaide, somebody inside the coffee shop anonymously purchased a plane ticket on her behalf, saving Denise the potentially deadly hike across the outback. She left that day with both physical and eternal security. Her trip to Adelaide was covered by a generous stranger, and the debt of her sins covered by "the gift of God … eternal life in Christ Jesus our Lord." (Romans 6:23)

Why do I share that story now? Well, two reasons:

First, I can't think of Sean Nolan without thinking about Broken Hill, Alice Springs, Kalgoorlie-Boulder, and all of the incredible ministry we've had together across Australia. As co-laborers for Christ, we've seen God move in wonderful ways and call many to repentance and salvation. These events—and these stories—serve as benchmarks of God's faithfulness.

Second, many of the themes of Sean's book, *The Way He Walked*, can also be found in Denise's redemptive story. God's love, forgiveness and salvation … His guiding hand … His purpose in our lives … walking alongside Him in our journey … the power of prayer … loving and serving others as Christ loves us… and—as followers of Christ—the importance of being prepared to say "Can I tell you about Jesus?" and relying on the Holy Spirit to speak through us in those tender moments.

As you begin this journey through *The Way He Walked*, I pray that you will be encouraged, challenged and uplifted in your faith. Through Sean's biblical insights, lean on God's Word and grow in it. Prepare your heart, and then be prepared to carry the great, eternal hope of Jesus Christ into your mission field.

May God bless each of you dearly,

Will Graham,
Billy Graham Evangelistic Association, Charlotte, USA.

SUPPORT FOR THIS BOOK

Sean Nolan has provided an accessible book of daily devotions covering 21 days, where he invites his readers to walk with God. Walking in the way of the Lord is redolent in both the Old and New Testaments, and is a mark of the Christian life—the way of love, which is to "walk in obedience to God's commands" (2 John 6).

Dr Glenn N Davies,
Former Anglican Archbishop of Sydney

Have you ever been asked to disciple someone? Or are you seeking spiritual refreshment but in both cases struggling to find resources? This little devotional book is for you. However, you have to be prepared to learn from deep verses in Scripture and historical Christian giants of the faith. As well, you'll need to have an open heart to "old" words like sin, repentance, loved, roots, death to self. If that is your desire you will truly be aided in your "walk before God" and positively rising with Him. On the journey you will reflect on personal issues like pain and confession. "*The Way He Walked*" is a practical and biblical guide in 101 discipleship. Its audience is those who walk the faith.

Rev. Dr Ross Clifford,
Executive Director NSW Council of Churches, Baptist Union NSW

I've known Sean for several years and admire how his life has always matched his message. From youth leading to evangelistic crusades, leadership conferences, Church planting, and PhD studies, he has pursued one thing—helping people walk with Jesus. In "*The Way He Walked*", he leads us through four vital movements: walking with Jesus, walking free from the past, walking as He walked, and walking others to Him. I highly recommend this book.

Pastor, Dr Richard Green,
Senior Minster C3 Church Ryde, C3 Reach

"*The Way He Walked – A 21-day Journey to Life as It Should Be*" by Dr Sean Nolan is a heartfelt and practical guide for believers seeking deeper intimacy with God. Whether new to faith or seasoned in the journey, readers are gently led through timeless truths — from grace and forgiveness to healing and restoration in Christ.

Each day invites transformation, not through striving, but by allowing the Holy Spirit to work within. Rooted in Scripture and written with clarity, this book points toward a life of growing holiness, joy, and love. As Paul writes in 2 Corinthians 5:14–15, "For Christ's love compels us…"

Let this journey draw you closer to God — and empower you to walk in the fullness of life He intends.

Commissioner Miriam Gluyas,
Salvation Army Australia Territorial Commander (National Leader)

I have known Sean and his beautiful family for several years.

In this time I have watched him develop and grow in his spiritual walk. Sean has a unique ability to connect with leaders right across the spectrum of Christendom, leaders from many denominations.

With a spirit of humility and grace he is forging out a ministry that will reach throughout all generations. His latest book, "*The Way He Walked*", is a "must read", purchase your copy today.

Pastor Kevin Brett,
Former Vice President, Australian Christian Churches, NSW

One of the great challenges of our contemporary culture is that we are chronically distracted. We all love the immediate access we have to media via our smart phones but research seems to suggest this is not making us smarter but in fact more shallow.

This impacts Christian discipleship. We need to help people build a consistent devotional life. Dr Sean Nolan's devotional book "*The Way He Walked*" will be a great help here. This gives people 21 devotions which combine Scripture, thoughts from key Christian leaders and pieces of insight and wisdom which will deepen the reader's faith and help their walk with Jesus.

This book is a chance to help each of us set a pattern over 21 days which will make a change to our distracted approach to life and personal faith.

Karl Faase,
CEO Olive Tree Media

Sean Nolan's book offers a deeply reflective 21-day walk examining our Christian lives and how God offers to grow us as Christians. But, it is not, as is too often the case with such writings, a "self-help book"! It is about *God,* who in Jesus has embraced us to himself, and made us his children. To quote: "God's love is the foundation all Christian teaching is built upon." The nature and reality of that love is what Sean walks us through with truthful insight and care. His explanations of the teaching of the Bible, his illustrations, and clarity with which he both outlines and leads us down the path God himself in Christ has given us, make this book very readable. Highly recommended.

Dr Robert Doyle,
Moore College, Sydney

In this short, accessible devotional, Sean Nolan is giving us a heartfelt call to move beyond just knowing about Jesus to truly knowing him in a deep, rich, soul-satisfying way. It is an invitation to know the living God through His Son Jesus and the Holy Spirit in true, intimate relationship. Along the way Sean proves to be a gentle, encouraging guide who nonetheless refuses to allow us to continue to deceive ourselves with false obedience, repentance, and faith by pointing us relentlessly to the joy of true surrender to God. If you are looking for a deeper, truer walk with God, this book will greatly bless you.

Pastor Tommy Briggs,
Gateway Baptist Church, Toledo, Ohio, USA
Professor of Bible & Theology, Revere Bible College, Monclova, Ohio

Sean and I have been friends for many years, so I have had the privilege of listening to the journey behind this book. What Sean has tapped into here is simple but key to living a life with Jesus. We tend to complicate how to walk with Jesus, but what this book shows us is that that is the problem: we try too much.

"*The Way He Walked*" takes us on a 21-day journey to hear God calling us into a life-changing relationship with him. One that will lead us out of the old and into the new.

Pastor Gabe Ortega,
Brookview Church, Seattle, USA

"*The Way He Walked*" provides an invitational journey to any believer, whether novice or seasoned, when it comes to the grace and heavenly trajectory that we are all invited into. With potent use of story, a life well lived, and acute observations within the gospels, Dr Sean Nolan provides a rich tapestry of Biblical truth that propels the believer forward. I was greatly enriched by engaging in this work.

Pastor Charlie Burke,
Exponential Australia

Since repentance is turning towards God (Acts 20:21; 1 Thess 1:9–10) and embracing the joy that the Lord Jesus Christ will one day share with us (Heb 12:1–2), this set of devotions gives us twenty-one days for our Heavenly Father to move us closer to his glorious future.

Professor Peter G. Bolt,
Director of Academic Strategy
Australian University College of Divinity

PREFACE

How this book came into existence

Two years ago, I attended a conference run by the late Tim Keller's ministry in Sydney on Church growth. As I sat there listening to the speakers, I felt the Holy Spirit arrest my attention through a simple Bible verse painted on the wall of the conference centre. The verse was: "*But seek first his kingdom and his righteousness, and all these things will be given to you as well*" (Matthew 6:33).

As I sat staring at this Scripture, God spoke to my heart. He quietly but firmly said to me that the answer to the powerlessness in the Church was not in better programs or any number of other things. The answer was in repentance (Acts 20:21). I realised in that moment that I was educated far beyond my level of repentance. My theological education had a place, but it had no power, as power comes from the Holy Spirit (2 Timothy 1:7) and he gives it to those who obey him (Acts 5:32).

When asked why God doesn't send revival sooner, Tim Keller once said, "the note of repentance just isn't there."[1] This thought made me realise that the main thing God was calling me to repent of was my longstanding efforts to change myself—which always failed. The one thing needed was the one thing I was so poor at, which was consistently walking with Jesus through his Word and prayer, allowing his grace and love to change my stubborn heart.[2]

Another thought, this time from Billy Graham, also caught my attention, "We can be convicted of sin—we can pray and confess our sin—we can repent—but the real test is our willingness to obey."[3] As I read this quote I could see that obedience was key to the Christian life, and, as a Christian leader, God was calling me to obey his command to be with him, to walk in his love so that his light and life could wash me and change me (2 John 6).[4]

This book is the outcome of this journey. I was a pastor, Church planter, denominational and Christian camping director, and had worked in evangelism with three separate international evangelists for decades and I still didn't "get it." This book is the pathway God took me on to wake me up and save me.

Perhaps the thing we forget the most is that God is the one who builds the Church. Jesus said, "I will build my church" (Matthew 16:18). In Acts 2:47 Luke says, "the Lord added to their number daily those who were being saved", and then Paul says of the Church, "God made it grow" (1 Corinthians 3:6, BSB). Notice these phrases: "I will build", "the Lord added", "God made it grow", this is a clear pattern in Scripture, and it

---

1 Tim Keller, "Remarks from Timothy Keller & Sinclair Ferguson."

2 2 Corinthians 5:14, Galatians 1:6-7, Philippians 2:13, Hebrews 8:10, 10:16.

3 Billy Graham, *The Holy Spirit*, 234.

4 See Charles Stanley's well known "30 Life Principles." Dr Stanley places "intimacy with God" before "obeying God."

shows us something key, which is that growth is God's job. If growth is God's job, then our task is to consistently walk with Jesus in belief and repentance. I wonder if this is what John the Baptist was getting at when he said, "*Bear fruit in keeping with repentance*" (Matthew 3:8, ESV).

The old missionaries used to say that fruit in the Christian life appears as "spontaneous growth" from a branch that is abiding in the vine (John 15:1-8). Friend, God knows how hard it is to be a Christian in this world. I want to encourage you by saying that as we get the basics of walking with God right, his great power becomes a reality and not a theory (Ephesians 1:19).

The goal of this 21-day journey is not to gain "theological insights" but to personally meet Jesus. As we learn to walk with Jesus in a consistent and healthy way, his love will drive out the old and bring forth the new—"*to know the love of Christ which passes knowledge; that you may be filled with all the fullness of God*" (Ephesians 3:19, NKJV).

Dr Sean Nolan, ThD,
The Great Commission Institute, Sydney, Australia.

"Teacher, which is the greatest commandment in the Law?"

Jesus replied: "'Love the Lord your God with all your heart and with all your soul and with all your mind.' This is the first and greatest commandment. And the second is like it: 'Love your neighbor as yourself.' All the Law and the Prophets hang on these two commandments."

Matthew 22:36-40

CONTENTS

PART ONE

God's invitation to walk with him

"When we walk with the Lord in the light of His word, what a glory He sheds on our way."

— Trust and Obey, John H. Sammis

DAY 1

Introducing walking with God

Many years ago, God spoke to me from Genesis 17:1-2 and said "*I am God Almighty; walk before me, and be blameless, that I may make my covenant between me and you, and may multiply you greatly*" (ESV). This little statement grabbed my attention and changed my life.

In the years following this encounter with the Lord, this verse hung on my wall and I would routinely stare at it wondering what exactly God meant by the phrase "*walk before me.*" The phrase "*God Almighty*" made perfect sense to me, as did the statement "*be blameless*" and the blessing promised, but the exact meaning of this little metaphor, "*walk before me*", seemed difficult to understand.

The question of what it means to walk before the Lord sits at the heart of this book, and it is the purpose of this 21-day journey to answer this question. To do this, the first place we need to turn is to Scripture. Throughout the Bible we see God inviting people to walk with him. We also see that God gives a variety of blessings to those who accept this invitation.

- Abraham was invited to "*walk before me faithfully and be blameless*" (Genesis 17:1).
- We see it recorded that Enoch and Noah "*walked faithfully with God*" (Genesis 5:22,24 and 6:9).
- God told Moses, "*My Presence will go with you*" — and the original Hebrew word for go means walk. (Exodus 33:14).
- David walked before God faithfully and God commands Solomon to do the same. (2 Chronicles 7:17).
- Isaiah tells us that those who hope in the Lord will find new strength, they will "*walk and not faint*" (Isaiah 40:31, ESV).
- The Gospels record that the disciples simply "*followed him*" (Jesus), which in the original Greek contains the idea of "walking the same road" as Jesus (Luke 5:11)[5]
- Paul commands the New Testament Church to "*walk by the Spirit", walk wisely*, and "*Walk as children of light*" (Galatians 5:16, Ephesians 5:15, and 5:8, ESV).
- John tells us that love is to "*walk in obedience to his commands*" and to "*walk as Jesus walked.*" (2 John 6, 1 John 2:6, BSB).

This personal invitation by God is truly unique. No other world religion claims to be visited directly by God himself. In the cluttered marketplace of world religions Christianity stands unique, as only in Christianity has God himself, in person, arrived and directly offered this invitation to humanity. We know this because the same Lord who appeared to Abraham, appeared in the homes and lives of ordinary people 2000 years ago (John 1:14). At the very start of the Gospels we see the Son of God invite his disciples to follow him.

---

5 Strongs Concordance, entry 190, akoloutheó.

At this point, it is important to clarify that following Jesus and walking before the Lord mean the same thing. Both ideas invite us to leave what we have been following—or walking before—to adopt Jesus as the new focus of our lives.

How this book works

Jesus' invitation was both simple and radical. In one instance, Jesus caught a fisherman's attention, told him not to be afraid, and that his life would have a new profound purpose. Scripture records this fisherman and his colleagues' response to Jesus' invitation, *"they pulled their boats up on shore, left everything and followed him"* (Luke 5:11). This disciple was Peter, and his simple yes to Jesus' invitation went on to change his life and the world.

This little story forms the structure of this book. The few steps that took place in Jesus' conversation with Peter are as follows: first, Jesus invited Peter to walk with him; second, Peter said yes by walking away from the past; third, Peter said a perpetual yes by daily walking with Jesus; and finally, Peter graduated from his walking-apprenticeship and spent the rest of his life walking others to Jesus. This produces four simple points for us:

1. God invites us to walk with him.
2. Jesus calls us to walk away from our past.
3. Learning to walk as Jesus walked.
4. Helping others walk with Jesus.

These points form the four sections of this 21-day journey, and each day has four simple elements:

1. Scripture.
2. A reading for the day.

3. A key thought to grasp, or believe.
4. An action to take.

In one sense, we can simply summarise the Christian walk as a "cycle" of study, belief, and action. We study the Word, we believe the Word, and then we act on the promises in the Word. This 21-day journey is centred on this simple threefold "cycle." As we build our life on the Word, we enter a relationship with Jesus— the ultimate change agent (John 6:63b, 15:5).

What the next 21 days looks like

I want you to know that none of the daily readings are long, they can all be read in around 10 minutes. The reason for this is that I know your life is busy, and I want you to have plenty of time to pray, journal and debrief with God over what has been discussed each day. The aim each day is to give you thoughts that will build your walk with God, not weigh you down with too much reading!

I also want to be open and honest with you about the fact that the next 21 days are designed to change you. I have been a pastor and Church planter in some of the tougher suburbs of Sydney for over 20 years, and have also worked extensively in evangelism. Alongside this, I cared for my hard and heavy dad for nearly 20 years as he slowly died, and my faithful Christian mother as she slowly died from ovarian cancer over a ten-year period. Through these experiences I have seen how difficult life can be, and also how beautiful even the most horrific situation can quickly become when people say yes to Jesus' invitation to walk with him.

Before my mum died, she would often tell the story of a rubbish dump in England that was turned into a beautiful park. The imagery of something so disgusting becoming a beautiful place of joy, laughter and community gave my mum endless hope as she battled cancer.

We may not know each other, but God who is the focus of this book knows you well. I believe that it is not a coincidence but rather a God-incidence that you are reading this book. Just like Abraham and Peter, you are being invited into a personal relationship with God. The God who walks among the stars wants to walk with us, and to make this happen we are invited to follow Jesus.

The prophet Daniel sought God for 21 days when he needed greater understanding about his life and situation (Daniel 10:3). Twenty-one days is three weeks; it's a short time. I believe God knows how busy life can be in the modern world, and if you will dedicate the next three weeks to walking with him through this journey, it may end up redirecting and redefining your entire life.

When Abraham walked with God a nation was born, when Noah walked with God a world was saved, when Moses walked with God a nation was delivered, when David walked with God a Kingdom was established, when Peter walked with Jesus the Church was born, and as we learn to walk with God our lives will never be the same.

If disbelief in God's ability to change and use you has already crept up into your heart, remember that it was not Abraham, Noah, Moses, David, nor Peter who did those things, it was God! And God wants to do new things through you!

We can be excited. As we seek to walk with God his power will make the impossible possible and the ordinary extraordinary. Enjoy the next 21 days!

Application overpage

Application

Scripture: "*When Abram was ninety-nine years old, the Lord appeared to him and said, 'I am God Almighty; walk before me faithfully and be blameless. Then I will make my covenant between me and you and will greatly increase your numbers.*'" Genesis 17:1-2

Key thought: Today is the first day of the rest of your life.

Action: Take note that Jesus has personally asked you to follow him. Verbally, out loud, respond to his invitation to you. That is, say to him, "Yes Lord, I accept your invitation to follow you."

DAY 2

Invited to walk in the Father's love

There is a story from the time of the Early Church about the last living Apostle, John. It is said that when John was very old his disciples would, with great struggle, carry his frail frame into the Church services. During these gatherings the aged servant of Jesus would say nothing other than, "Little children, love one another." The congregation members eventually became annoyed by John's repetitive words and asked him, "Teacher, why do you always say this?" John's reply was, "Because it is the Lord's commandment and if it alone is kept, it is sufficient."[6] If John was in our modern hurried world, perhaps he would simply say, "I teach love, because that is what the Master taught us."

Established in love

The Gospel is a message of change through love. Paul prayed for the Church in Ephesus that they would be *"rooted and established in love"* so that they

[6] The Fathers of the Church, *St Jerome Commentary of Galatians*, commentary on chapter 6:10, page 260. I believe the next line is a rephrasing I once read/heard, I cannot recall the source and apologise to the mystery author.

could *"be filled to the measure of all the fullness of God"* (Ephesians 3:17-19). This simple prayer teaches us something very profound about our lives, which is that what we are planted in matters.

The first home my wife and I bought sat across from a flood plain which would frequently fill with rushing water when it rained. In the middle of this area sat a lone, large, gum tree. The frequent rushing water had eroded the ground around the base of the tree and, to the naked eye, it looked rather unstable. After large storms I would often go out the front expecting to find that this mighty tree had fallen victim to its circumstances. But it never did. The reason why this tree never fell was that its roots took up the same area underground as the visible leaves did above. The tree was rooted and established in the earth around it and no matter what came against it, it stood.

This gum tree reminds us of Jesus' parable about the man who built his house on the rock (Matthew 7:24-27). In this parable Jesus said that everyone who hears his teaching and implements it in their lives is like the man who built his house on the rock, or, they are like a gum tree which buried its roots deep into the earth. In Jesus' parable the foundation holds the building in place, likewise the key thing to notice about the gum tree is that it's not the roots that hold onto the soil, it is the soil that holds the roots in place. When we build our life on the love of God we are building it on God's gracious offer to hold us and keep us safe from the temptations and sins of this world.

I don't want to get too technical here, but in Christian theology a key thing the Holy Spirit comes to do is fill us with God's love, Paul explains this when he says, "*God's love has been poured out into our hearts through the Holy Spirit, who has been given to us*" (Romans

5:5).[7] It is good to notice that when the Apostle John tells us to "*walk in love*", it corresponds to the Apostle Paul telling us to "*walk in the Spirit*" (2 John 6, Galatians 5:25, NKJV).

The Holy Spirit is the soil, our walk the roots, and our lives the fruitful tree. The mature truth is that you choose where your roots grow. You can either put your roots down daily into the Spirit of God through the Word of God, or you can put your roots down into the worries of this world. If you put roots down into God this way, you are building your life on his love (1 John 4:16).

Our Christian life is a shared responsibility, God has provided the soil for us to grow in, but we must choose to plunge our life—our roots—into this soil.

A loving Father

At the start of The Lord's Prayer, Jesus tells us to come to God as we would to a loving and trustworthy father. Based on this idea, Christian theology has taught for centuries that our walk with God is to be seen through a father-to-child relationship.[8]

God is a loving Father and no matter what we have done we are always to see ourselves as loved children. This is nowhere better seen than in the story of The Prodigal Son, which could also be called the story of the loving father, or the waiting father. There is a key moment in this story where the son "*came to his senses*", this phrase is also translated as "*he came to himself*" (Luke 15:17, ESV). What this means is that the son remembers who he is, because of whose he is. The son remembered that he was the loved son of a

---

7 Augustine famously wrote that the Holy Spirit "inflames" us to the love of God. Augustine, *On The Trinity*, book 15, chapter 17, section 31, see also book 15, chapter 19, section 37.

8 John Calvin, *Institutes of the Christian Religion*, Book three, Chapter 20, Sections 36-39. Karl Barth, *The Christian Life*, pages 43, 49.

loving father. Upon this realisation the son decides to stop walking before his failure and to return to walking in his father's loving provision and protection. The son, weighed down by guilt decides to return home, but what he doesn't anticipate is that his father is already waiting for him, at the gate! Before the son says a word, the father runs to him, throws his arms around him and kisses him. Then the loving, understanding father quickly restores him into his household, and upon the son's confession, moves on from the matter.

This story teaches us something foundational for our walk with the Lord, which is that we need to accept by faith that we are a loved child of God (Galatians 5:6). When we do this, we will join the prodigal son and walk towards our loving Father, quickly finding ourselves wrapped in his embrace.

An important point here is that our walk begins by faith. The story doesn't say that the son saw the father, it says that the father saw the son coming and ran to him. You may not see God, but you can turn to him by faith, assured that he sees you and that he will run to you.

In the ancient culture it was highly undignified and even inappropriate for an older respected man to run in public. Jesus is making a point in this story by including the detail that the father "*ran*" to his son. You may feel like your situation is so murky that there is no way God would embrace you. This biblical story dispels that and shows you that God is willing to enter even the dirtiest situation to save.

Friend, you also need to know that it doesn't matter where you are reading this, or from where you are beginning your walk back to the Father. You may be a pastor reading this in the Church office, or you may be reading this in a nightclub. Your current location doesn't determine your destiny. What matters is where you are walking, which is either further into your failures or towards a new future with your loving Father. The son had been feeding unclean pigs and would have been covered in their filth. For a Jewish father to embrace someone in this situation broke all societal and religious norms. God is willing to embrace, clean, forgive, and give a glorious fresh future to anyone who walks toward him (1 John 1:9).

A loving diagnosis

The evangelist Billy Graham often called sin a disease. God saying we are sinners in need of salvation is not something to get offended over, it is something to be thankful about. Imagine for a moment a doctor who knew someone was terminally ill and had the cure for this sickness but never told the person either of these things. This doctor would be seen as a cruel and selfish person. In a similar way, God showing us our sin and offering us the cure is not mean or condemning, it is kind and loving.

God is inviting us to have our lives changed by his love. This love calls us out of the misery of sin, and into a new life of light, love, and purpose. The Bible says that God's love is the instigator of all his dealings with us (Ephesians 1:4b-5). Everything God allows, does, or doesn't do in our lives is done through the lens of his love.

The key lesson we learn from The Prodigal Son story is that just as Jesus' love is to be the focus of our walk with him, Jesus makes loving us the focus of his walk with us. Like the "undignified" father who ran to embrace his unclean son, Jesus will break societal norms to find you, love you, and change you.

Application

Scripture: *"But blessed is the one who trusts in the Lord, whose confidence is in him. They will be like a tree planted by the water that sends out its roots by the stream. It does not fear when heat comes; its leaves are always green. It has no worries in a year of drought and never fails to bear fruit."* Jeremiah 17:7-8

Key thought: You are loved by God.

Action: Just as the prodigal son "*came to himself*", accept in your heart and mind that you are the loved child of a loving Father. Spend time in prayer meditating on this thought.

DAY 3

Invited to walk like the Son

Today we will look at three different thrones which give us three different sources for how we can live our lives. One throne gives us religious glory, another gives God's glory, and the final one produces worldly glory.

A throne of golden splendour (religious glory)

There is a story in the Old Testament that describes the time the Queen of Sheba came to meet with King Solomon. This story is captured through a life-size painting in an art gallery in the heart of Sydney. The painting brings the story to life and you can imagine being the Queen of Sheba as she enters the throne room of Solomon.

When the Queen of Sheba came into Solomon's presence, her eyes would have immediately been drawn to the extravagant throne that he sat on. She would have seen Solomon sitting on a large golden throne with two life-size gold lions on either side of him. As she walked up to meet him, she would have had to walk past a further twelve golden lions that sat on the steps which ascended upwards to the king. The Bible says of this incredible golden throne, that "*nothing like it had ever been made for any other kingdom*" (1 Kings 10:20).

The purpose of this throne was to display the glory that Solomon possessed as king. As the King of Israel, Solomon chose to create this spectacular throne for himself as he felt like it represented his power and might. When we fast forward a thousand or so years, we see a very different type of king adorn a very different type of throne, which in turn represents a very different kingdom.

A throne of crimson cedar (God's glory)

Father God chose thrones for his Son that he felt communicated heavenly glory (John 19:11). The first throne we see associated with Jesus is his Father's throne in Heaven. The Bible gives us glimpses into the vista that awaits the redeemed believer when they enter the Kingdom of God. The writer of Hebrews talks about the Temple of God that is "*not part of this creation*", and that within this Temple Jesus has a "*glorious throne*" (Hebrews 9:11, Matthew 19:28). What is, however, even more incredible than both Jesus' eternal throne and King Solomon's golden throne, is the throne God chose on Earth.

It is incredible to think that Jesus chose to make a bloodied cedarwood Cross the place where God's glory is most clearly seen. It was on this Cross that the sacrificial loving nature of God was broadcast to all creation, showing us that real glory is about serving and not being served (Mark 10:45). Solomon showed his glory through a throne of golden splendour, but Jesus showed God's glory on a throne of bloodied cedar. On the Cross, Jesus redefined glory, and just as it was said that nothing like Solomon's throne was ever

made in any other kingdom, nothing like the act of Jesus on the Cross has ever been seen in any other kingdom.

The thrones of today (worldly glory)

Our world offers us plenty of modern-day thrones. We see thrones in the corporate world, celebrity culture, sport, politics and even in our religious institutions. These may not be literal chairs that people sit on, but they have the same function as the throne Solomon made for himself—which is to show the glory we see in ourselves.

It is interesting to contrast the imagery from yesterday of our Christian walk as a tree that is putting roots down into God, with the three thrones discussed so far today. The thing about roots is that they gain their nourishment from the soil that they sit within. This means that what we put our roots into determines what will be in us (Luke 11:34). The three thrones we have looked at today offer us three sources of nourishment for our lives and in turn three very different identities.

Source one: the world

First, we can choose to put our roots down into the thrones, stages, offices, and institutions of the world to be sustained by them. My dad worked for a large bank in Australia for 39 years. He started as a bank teller in regional Australia and worked his way up to a senior management role in the head office. One day, after 39 years of service, a young administrator came in and informed him and his entire department that they were no longer required. My dad had placed much of his identity in this role and when it was removed he was lost. Fame, position, and power can come and go so quickly. If we have our roots planted in these things then we are destined to be disappointed. Everyone can remember who won an election or sporting event the morning after, but rarely the year after. And only that which is done for Jesus will be remembered in eternity (Matthew 7:24-27).

Source two: works for God

Second, we can put our roots down into our work for God. This can be tricky to discuss as we are commanded by God to serve him and to make our service to him personal. A Christian's ministry doesn't begin when they interact with someone out in society, it begins in the prayer closet. This makes Christian service intensely personal (Romans 12:1-2). This noted, our service to God is not who we are, it is what we do because of who we are. The Bible tells us that our identity is to be in the fact that we are a loved child of Almighty God (1 John 3:1). I have known many Christians, pastors and congregation members who have had great struggle because a ministry came to an end. What we must remember is that our service to God will change and even come to an end one day, but our status as a child of God never changes and never comes to an end. We need to base our lives in that which is permanent and eternal (Colossians 3:1-2).

Source three: Jesus

Third, we can choose to put our roots down into our relationship with Jesus. Jesus said that we are not to see ourselves as servants, but rather as his friends (John 15:15). One of Jesus' closest friends the Apostle John, told us, "*Whoever claims to live in him must live as Jesus did*" (1 John 2:6). We see in the life of Jesus the opposite of both the worldly approach and even the religious way of walking. Jesus could have rebuilt the throne of Solomon and then some, but instead he taught that kind of glory was fleeting (Matthew 24:2).

Jesus located glory in self-sacrifice, giving, and service. John begins his Gospel by telling us that they have "*seen his glory*" (John 1:14). John is not talking about Jesus on his glorious eternal throne, but rather, the Son of God making a bloodied wooden Cross glorious. At the Cross we see the glory of God, in that he would allow himself to be sacrificially crucified for our salvation.[9] The world and even religion sees glory in dominating other people, the Bible teaches that glory comes from serving others (Mark 10:45).

Living for God's glory

Humans are made to give and not get worship, we are made to bow before God's throne, not be on a throne. When we build our lives on a desire for worldly or religious glory we are looking to get worship. When we build our lives on glorifying Father God, like Jesus did, we are giving God glory. The Christian who has put their roots down into a life of giving God glory is walking the way Jesus walked.

When we live for our own glory, all our life's achievements end when we die. When we live for God's glory, our life produces "*an eternal weight of glory beyond all comparison*" (2 Corinthians 4:17, ESV). God is inviting you to give up the pursuit of your personal glory and to make your heart's desire to glorify his name (Isaiah 26:8, NLT). When we commit to this, living for God's glory proves far more satisfying than living for our own glory.

[9] John 12:27-28, 17:1-5, 17:20-24.

Application

Scripture: "*For even the Son of Man did not come to be served, but to serve, and to give his life as a ransom for many.*"
Mark 10:45

Key thought: Jesus invites us to live for a cause far greater than ourselves.

Action: Think through how you can use your life and talents to show the glory of God. Write down some practical steps you can take to further your relationship with Jesus by serving others, knowing that when you do this, you are walking in the way of Jesus.

DAY 4

Invited to walk in the Holy Spirit's power

In my backyard is a vibrant rose bush which flowers all year round. This rose bush was originally my mother's and when I go out and smell the large red fragrant flowers it produces, I am immediately reminded about her. My mother died ten years ago, but her memory vividly lives on through these roses. The mere sight of them immediately transports my mother's love and kindness out of the past and into the present.

This simple story is an example of how the Holy Spirit works in our lives.[10] In the same way these roses are not my mum but remind me about her, the Holy Spirit is not Jesus, but he always points us to Jesus.[11]

---

[10] No human illustration can ever convey the reality of the Holy Spirit's relationship to both Jesus and the Father, and then us. This is a simple pastoral illustration.

[11] In John 14-16 Jesus teaches that the Holy Spirit comes to illuminate us to the truth that we can be reconciled back to our loving heavenly Father through faith in Jesus' death and resurrection for us.

Another illustration of how the Spirit shows us Jesus is seen through the example of both clear and frosted glass. The Spirit is like "clear" glass in the sense that he enables us to see Jesus fully. However, the Spirit can also deal with us like "frosted" glass, in the sense that the image of Christ we gain through the Spirit also shows us something of who the Holy Spirit is himself.[12]

Jesus tells us in John 3 that there is a mysterious side to how the Holy Spirit works, but there is no mystery surrounding what the Spirit is looking to achieve in our lives. Jesus says in John 14:26 that the Holy Spirit will "*teach you all things and will remind you of everything I have said.*" This tells us that the Holy Spirit comes into our lives to teach us how to walk like Jesus (1 John 2:6, ESV).

An insight into how this works comes when we consider the basic truth of Christianity, which is that Jesus is both God and man. Jesus lived with one foot in Heaven and one in the world. The Holy Spirit comes to help us learn to live like Jesus, in the sense that we are to learn to live our earthly lives through heavenly power.

As we follow the Bible's teaching, the power of the Holy Spirit makes it possible for us to know Jesus personally and intimately. It is important to realise that we walk with Jesus through the Holy Spirit.[13]

Power from another place

In his exchange with Pilate before his crucifixion, Jesus says *"my kingdom is from another place"* (John 18:36). This teaches us that the power we need to walk with God comes to us from a place we can't see. For many years

---

[12] This analogy is from my former doctoral supervisor, Dr Robert Doyle of Moore Theological College. He uses the words transparent and translucent.

[13] This is why the Bible calls the Holy Spirit the Spirit of Jesus Christ, Philippians 1:19, Acts 16:7, Galatians 4:6, Romans 8:9. And just as the Spirit comes to point us to Jesus, Jesus came to point us to the Father, John 12:49-50, 14:6.

a picture hung in the Billy Graham Association office in Australia of Dr Graham with the words written on it, "'*not by might nor by power, but by my Spirit,' says the LORD Almighty*" (Zechariah 4:6). While I worked there, this served as a reminder that the Christian who walks in the power of the Holy Spirit does so not by any human capacity, but by simple childlike faith.

Jesus said that unless you "*change and become like little children, you will never enter the kingdom of heaven*" (Matthew 18:3). Consider how a little child doesn't doubt the ability of their father or mother to provide for them, they live in total trust and dependence upon their parents. We are called to approach walking with Jesus in the Christian life this same way. We can try to live each day of our Christian life by walking in reliance upon ourselves or other humans to provide for us, or we can rely on the Holy Spirit who leads us to the Gospel of Christ, which changes everything. A simple example of this follows.

God cares

When I first entered Bible College, I worked at a department store in the centre of Sydney. I was assigned to help run the men's suiting department and quickly found myself in need of a new suit. My green, polyester, eight-button school formal suit no longer fitted me and was no longer fit for civilised society! As a young Bible College student, I had no spare money and found myself praying to God to help me buy a new suit. I distinctly remember the Holy Spirit reminding me about the Lord's teaching where he said:

> *"And why do you worry about clothes? See how the flowers of the field grow. They do not labor or spin. Yet I tell you that not even Solomon in all his splendor was dressed like one of these. If that is how God clothes the grass of the field, which is here*

> *today and tomorrow is thrown into the fire, will he not much more clothe you—you of little faith?"* (Matthew 6:28-30)

I remember this passage challenging me about two things. First, was that God cared about my need for a new suit. This was hard to accept because so many other people's needs seemed much more important. Second, I was challenged to trust God to provide, which he did. God opened the eyes of someone close to me and they offered to help me buy the suit, and a pair of shoes! I realise this is a simple example, but if we don't trust God in the small things we will never trust him in the big things. Trust in the power and willingness of God to provide through the Holy Spirit is like a muscle, one which needs to be exercised to get stronger.

A real heart-experience of being loved by God

The above story leads us to the truth that our walk with the Lord cannot be theoretical, it must be personal. Tim Keller once said that we must "ask the Holy Spirit to help us experience our theology."[14] When Tim Keller said this, he was discussing a quote from the English theologian John Owen who said, "get an *experience* of the power of the gospel… in and upon your own hearts, or all your profession is an expiring thing."

Paul tells us that when we "*know*" the love of Christ we will "*be filled with all the fullness of God*" (Ephesians 3:19, ESV). The Greek word for know in this verse means "to know, especially through personal experience."[15]

On day two we looked at Paul's teaching that the Holy Spirit offers to fill us with God's love (Romans 5:5).[16] This led to the realisation that the

---

[14] Tim Keller, *Prayer: Experiencing Awe and Intimacy with God.* Page 10. John Owen's quote is in this article by Keller, sentence tense adjusted.

[15] Strongs Concordance entry 1097.

[16] Augustine famously wrote that the Holy Spirit "inflames" us to the love of God. Augustine, *On The Trinity*, book 15, chapter 17, section 31, see also book 15, chapter

Apostle John's direction to "*walk in love*" corresponds to the Apostle Paul telling us to "*walk in the Spirit*" (2 John 6, Galatians 5:25, NKJV). The evangelist D. L. Moody explained this when he said, "it is the work of the Holy Spirit to impart love."[17]

Today we want to ask the Holy Spirit to fulfil this scriptural promise and impart God's love into our lives, afresh and anew, by faith.

The above quotes from John Owen and Tim Keller remind us that our knowledge of God's Spirit and love cannot be an academic thing, rather the Christian walk is a real-life experience of being loved by God.[18] John Piper has some further helpful thoughts on this:

> "God's love poured into your heart is not the same as God's love proven to your mind. God's love poured into your heart is a real heart-experience of being loved by God. God's love proven to your mind is the conclusion of an argument, with or without the sweetness of feeling loved by God in the heart. I want you to know this sweetness. I want you to enjoy this gift: the outpouring of the love of God in your hearts."[19]

The Gospel is a message of change through love, and this change happens through the love of Christ being poured into our hearts through the Holy Spirit (Romans 5:5). We get a window into how this works when God showed himself to Elijah. In this story, God was not in the sensational earthquake or fire, but he was in the "*gentle whisper*" or "*still small voice*"

19, section 37.

[17] D. L. Moody, *Secret Power, The Right Overflow*, 20. Language modernised.

[18] See also the ending of this article by Michael Keller, *My Dad (Tim Keller) Listened to History to Speak the Gospel*, The Gospel Coalition US.

[19] John Piper, *How to Experience the Outpouring of God's Love,* Desiring God. Emphasis added.

(1 Kings 19:12, NKJV). God conforms to Scripture, and Scripture tells us that the experience of being loved by God can be described as "*a still small voice*", deeply and powerfully proving to our hearts that we are loved by God.

We serve a living Christ not a dead Christ, and he is more than willing to touch your heart with his wellspring of love that comes from the Cross. From this place of inner rest, he teaches you how to walk in newness of life (Romans 6:4).

Application

Scripture: *"God's love has been poured out into our hearts through the Holy Spirit, who has been given to us."*
Romans 5:5

Key thought: "The Spirit brings us to God and God to us"—Augustine.

Action: Ask God in prayer to give you a real heart-experience of his love for you and others (John 15:17).

DAY 5

Invited to die (to self)

In the story of The Prodigal Son there is a tense exchange between the father and the older brother after the wayward son returns. Basically, the older brother protests the father's generous love and the father pleads with him to have a change of heart. The exchange ends with the statement, "*But we had to celebrate and be glad, because this brother of yours was dead and is alive again; he was lost and is found*" (Luke 15:32, emphasis added).

This simple statement gives us an understanding of how God views our existence here on Earth, which is that we are not alive, but rather dead. I imagine that this could be both confusing and confronting to hear. Confusing in the sense that we are obviously physically alive, which makes us wonder what exactly the Bible means by calling us dead. And confronting, as calling someone else "dead" can be seen as a rather odd thing to say.

The Bible explains our dead state when it says, "*you were dead in your transgressions and sins, in which you used to live*", going on to say, "*God, who is rich in mercy, made us alive with Christ*" (Ephesians 2:1-2,4-5). Jesus himself explains this point when he says that those who follow him have "*crossed over from death to life*" (John 5:24).

We all have areas of our lives that we wish to see move from being dead to alive, and the way in which we cross over from death to life is clearly seen in the story of Lazarus. The Bible says that Jesus simply called to Lazarus in a loud voice, "*come out*!", and then "*the dead man came out*" (John 11:43-44). Friend, just as Jesus called to Lazarus, he is calling to you today: "*come out*!"

Only you and God know what it is that you need to "come out" from today. Maybe it's complete spiritual death because you have never trusted Jesus as your personal Saviour. Or maybe it's a lifelong sinful habit. Or yet still, it could be a past rejection, hurt, or failure that has plagued you for decades. While our individual situations vary, the solution doesn't. Jesus called to Lazarus and he had a choice, stay in the darkness of death or get up and walk towards the one calling to him.

Living because of love

The first step of walking towards Jesus is to walk away from what the Bible calls our "*old self*", which is controlled by two things, sinful desires and unhealthy mindsets (Ephesians 4:22-23). If we return to the story of The Prodigal Son we can see these two points at work.[20]

The prodigal son was driven to waste his father's wealth and his own inheritance through "*wild living*", but quickly found that "*he began to be in need.*" There is a lot that can be said here, but the main points are that both sin and the friends we make when we live sinfully are poor companions. Sin is enjoyable for a season, but the joy of sin quickly gives way to the sting of sin. Sin is the opposite of righteous living. Sin can feel good in the

[20] Luke 15:11-32.

moment, but it always produces a negative long-term outcome. Righteous living, however, often feels hard in the moment, but produces a positive long-term outcome. The Bible tells us to judge sin by its deathly outcome, not its momentary enjoyment.

The story of The Prodigal Son also demonstrates to us the power of our thinking to either destroy or build our future. As the prodigal son was enduring the negative effects of his sin the Bible says "*he went and hired himself out to a citizen of that country.*" Later on we see that he "*came to his senses*" and returned to his father. This is an important point because at this stage of the story it was no longer sin that was keeping him in poverty, it was his mindset.

The Prodigal Son had to stop living based off what he had done wrong, and what had been done to him, and return to drawing his identity from his father's love. When the prodigal son realised that his sin didn't cancel his father's love he returned home.

Turn and take your journey

> "It's not death to die."
>
> Hudson Taylor

Jesus said, *"unless a kernel of wheat falls to the ground and dies, it remains only a single seed. But if it dies, it produces many seeds"* (John 12:24). The mature truth is that we need to decide to die to sin and old mindsets, and when we do God uses the death of our old life to seed a new life. At this point_it is important to understand that the death of the old is not something we can accomplish on our own, it is a partnership between us and the Holy Spirit.

In Galatians 2:20 Paul says, "*I have been crucified with Christ.*" The Greek word Paul uses here is *sustauroó.* This word is in what's called the passive voice in the original Greek language, which means that Paul is not the one performing the action. Paul is saying that someone else crucified his old life, which is God. This teaches us that we must invite the Lord into our life to crucify the old life, so that a new one can begin.

God said to the Israelites as they journeyed to the promised land *"You have stayed long enough at this mountain. Turn and take your journey"* (Deuteronomy 1:6b-7a, ESV). Friend, you have stayed at a place defined by your past long enough. It's time to turn and take your journey towards resurrection life, and this road begins at the Cross.

The prodigal son's moment of realisation happened when he burned with hunger so strongly that the Bible says he "*was longing to be fed with the pods that the pigs ate*" (Luke 15:16). It cannot be overstated how desperate a Jewish man of that era would have to be to even touch a pig, let alone eat what they were eating. The prodigal son realised that he was living far outside of his position and potential. Upon this realisation he didn't sit down and draw up a strategy to reinvent himself; he went back to the place his position and provision came from, his father.

It's time to stop walking before your past mistakes or past efforts to eradicate sin from your life. Jesus came into the world to do the will of God <u>for you,</u> and the Holy Spirit has been sent into the world to accomplish the will of God <u>in you</u> (Hebrews 10:5-7, 15-16). You are not alone. God is with you and willing to help you in miraculous ways as you say yes to his call to walk out of the past and into the future.

God doesn't cause our suffering, but he does allow it, and the Bible tells us that he does this for a good purpose (Romans 8:28). You can't plant a vineyard until you have properly prepared the ground. If you leave rubbish, rocks and weeds in the land nothing of value will grow on the vine. God takes away the old to establish something new. This teaches us that the first great gift of the Gospel is not the power to rise but the power to die—the power to see past our hurts and for long-standing sins to lose their hold over us.

Many years ago, the Early Church theologian Augustine wrote about how past hurts, rejections, and failures can grip us in the present. We can be happily going about our morning routine and then, like a bolt of lightning, a negative memory can flood into our minds and derail our day. Our past hurts, rejections, and failures often plague our present lives, and if left unchecked, old hurts will wreak havoc on us. The same is true of sin.

God wants to free you from the chains of the past. Maybe you have tried thousands of times to be free from the power of a past situation or to kick sin out of your life. Today, I want you to stop trying and ask God to do it for you (Philippians 2:13). To do this, consider praying this prayer, one adapted from Charles Stanley's preaching ministry:

Prayer: Today, I'm asking the same Holy Spirit that saved me to enable me to die to sin, and to break the mental chains from my past hurts, rejections, and failures. Lord Jesus, change me. Lord Jesus, take the old and bring the new. Lord Jesus, make your will my desire. Lord Jesus, burn the self out of me and burn your mighty love into me. I want to live a godly life, a holy life, one that's pleasing and honourable to you Lord.

Now, I pray my new life will bring you joy, Lord, and that you will enable me to share this awesome message with others. I pray this in Jesus' name, amen.

Application

Scripture: *"Very truly I tell you, whoever hears my word and believes him who sent me has eternal life and will not be judged <u>but has crossed over from death to life</u>."* John 5:24, emphasis added

Key thought: Death is the gateway to life.

Action: Today, spend meaningful time in prayer, inviting the Holy Spirit into your life to crucify the old and birth the new (John 12:24, Galatians 2:20).

DAY 6

Invited to rise

Yesterday we learnt that we are all desperate for something to die (end) in our lives. Whether it be a long-term sinful habit, or the influence of a past hurt, rejection or failure, we all have something that we want gone from our life.

Trying to remove these things is a trillion-dollar industry in our modern world: physicians, counsellors, personal trainers, dietitians, beauticians and all sorts of other professions are dedicated to removing the old in the hope that new things will grow.

The truth is that for a time we can use our willpower to hold back unwanted habits and thoughts, but we will soon find that our best efforts begin to spring leaks. The Bible teaches that self-control, renewal, and resurrection don't originate from us, rather it is the fruit of walking with the Spirit. The ability to truly change is a gift from God.[21]

[21] Philippians 2:13, Galatians 5:22-23, Romans 12:1-2, Hebrews 10:5-7, 15-16.

The four stages of resurrection

Through the Gospel God awakens us to an existence radically different to what we have known. A perfect example of this is the caterpillar. The caterpillar instinctively knows that something is wrong, that it is not who it should be. The caterpillar is awakened to another potential and begins to take action to make this possible. It builds a cocoon and enters it, knowing that in this place it will die, but the death of the caterpillar is not the end, for a butterfly is about to be born.

In Romans 12:2 Paul tells us to be "*transformed.*" The original Greek word used in this verse (metamorphoó) is the same as the word used to describe the transfiguration of Jesus (Matthew 17:2). Through the Christian walk, God is transfiguring us, which simply means to change us into the image of his Son (Romans 8:9). Like the caterpillar, this process involves the end of the old so that a beautiful new thing can begin. God doesn't want you crawling through life, that's what serpents do. God wants you to be transformed so that you can "*soar on wings like eagles*" (Isaiah 40:31).

One of the best books written on the biblical process for moving from crawling to soaring in the Christian life is by Robert Mulholland. In his book, he discusses four stages for the Christian life, which we will use today to outline four stages of resurrection.[22]

Stage one: awakening

This is the initial stage of resurrection. In this stage, God awakens you to how unlike him you are. This involves two key things: an awakening to how holy God is and an awakening to how unholy you are.

---

22 M. Robert Mulholland, *Invitation to Journey*, part eight.

Many well-intentioned Christians assume that they are past this step when they are not. Billy Graham reminds us that it is possible to repent without obeying: "We can be convicted of sin—we can pray and confess our sin—we can repent—but the real test is our willingness to obey."[23] The way we know we have truly awakened to God's holiness and our unholiness is that we desire to radically change, which leads to the next step.

Stage two: purification[24]

When we have awakened to how unlike God we are, we learn to walk with him, which brings our behaviours, attitudes and desires into harmony with who Scripture tells us Jesus is (Galatians 5:16). The Apostle John tells us that "*Whoever claims to live in him must live as Jesus did*" (1 John 2:6). It is in this purification stage that we learn to live in total submission to the Father's will, just like Jesus did (Philippians 2:8). This involves leaving our own desires behind and taking up a lifestyle of sacrifice and service to God and others (Matthew 16:24).

Simply said, we are purified by the Holy Spirit leading us to the Gospel of Christ, which changes everything. Remembering that it is Jesus' blood that purifies us from all sin (Hebrews 9:22, 10:14).

As we become purified, we can enter the next stage of our resurrection journey, which is illumination.

Stage three: illumination

At this third stage we come to understand that God's love is the engine that drives out the old life and fuels the growth of a new life. Being illuminated to this truth results in us going from doing righteous works to try and be

23 Billy Graham, *The Holy Spirit*, 234.

24 Mulholland calls this stage "purgation", I changed the word to modernise it.

acceptable to God, to doing righteous works because we are accepted by God. This represents a radically new life structure of being with God to then do for God. Not the other way around of doing for God in the hope of being able to be with God. Another way to describe this stage is to say that we move from having knowledge about God, to knowing God.

The Apostle John calls this abiding in God's love (John 15:9), and the Apostle Paul calls it living by the grace of Christ (Galatians 1:6). These are two ways of describing the same thing, which is God's presence and activity in our lives being the genesis (beginning) of personal holiness and fruitfulness in the Christian life (John 15:8). Simply said, holiness and fruitfulness in the Christian life are received not achieved (Romans 4:5, 7:4).

Stage four: union

On day two we said that the Gospel is a message of change through love. As we become illuminated to this truth in stage three, we grow closer to both Jesus Christ and his purpose. This does not mean we never sin again, it simply means that we know what it is to walk with God, and the result of this is that the things of the world become increasingly unappealing to us.

This is also the place where we begin to understand that all we need to do to find our life's purpose is merge our God given talents and passions with the Great Commission. We see Jesus effortlessly do this with Peter when he merges his love for fishing with the Great Commission. Peter goes from being a fisherman to being a fisher of men (Matthew 4:18-19).

When we know the love of Christ and know our unique purpose and place in his Kingdom we live fulfilled lives. Lives that bring him much fruit and glory (John 15:8).

Resurrection moves at the pace of obedience

The four stages discussed today are all aspects of the one mighty resurrection Jesus brings to us. Progress through these stages can be slow at times in life, but we must remember that growth in the Christian walk moves at the pace of obedience. This can be rephrased to say that resurrection moves at the pace of obedience. James 1:22 reminds us that obedience is not just hearing and talking about the commands of God, obedience is doing the commands of God. The mature truth is that anything but compliance with what God asks of us is a movement toward counterfeit Christianity.

Jesus' life was hallmarked by abiding in the Father's love through obeying him (John 15:10), and the Holy Spirit works to repeat the life (or obedience) of Jesus in us. In each of the four stages mentioned today the Spirit leads us to obey in a different way, so that we can become more like Jesus.

The honest truth is that the resurrection journey discussed today could bring a mild discouragement to us, as we could feel like it will take forever to become like Christ. The truth is that the Christian walk is a lifelong process, but it is also true that we can move forward quickly if we are willing to let the axe fall at the base of the tree (Matthew 3:10, John 15:2).[25] Psalm 81:13-14 reminds us of how willing God is to act for us:

> *"If my people would only listen to me,*
> *if Israel would only follow my ways,*
> *how quickly I would subdue their enemies*
> *and turn my hand against their foes!"*

Will you today obey God's call to awaken to his holiness and your unholiness? Will you obey God's call to have your life purified from sin

[25] See, Ruth Paxton, *Rivers of Living Water*, page 100. Both this book by Paxton and *Life on the Highest Plane* are well worth reading. As is most missionary biography.

and self? Maybe God is illuminating you to a new life of being with him to then do for him—will you say yes to this invitation?

Our constant "yes" to God makes us like Christ. And when we are "*united with him in a death like his, we will certainly also be united with him in a resurrection like his*" (Romans 6:5). And remember, the butterfly was born when the caterpillar consented to change.

Application

Scripture: *"For to me, to live is Christ and to die is gain"* Philippians 1:21

Key thought: Obedience always brings blessing—Charles Stanley.

Action: Identify which of the four stages best describes your current walk with the Lord. Talk to God about this.

DAY 7

Invited to walk with purpose

Over the past six days we have looked at God's invitation to walk with him. We got to know each member of the Trinity (days 2-4) and then unpacked how the death and resurrection of Jesus touches our lives (days 5-6). Tomorrow we will shift to look at Jesus' invitation to walk away from our past, but before we do this, we will spend today understanding what it means to live with eternal purpose on Earth. This is important because if we understand God's eternal purpose for our lives, we will gain fresh motivation to walk away from our past lifestyle.

> *"He has put eternity into man's heart."*
>
> Ecclesiastes 3:11

In the Parable of the Sower, Jesus describes the person who hears and accepts the Word of God as someone whose life is "*good soil*" (Mark 4:1-20). This means that when we say "yes" to God, he enters our lives and gives us the ability to bear fruit for his eternal Kingdom. In the Parable of the Sower, the first stage of this process is hearing the Word of God. Another way to say this is that we must hear God calling to us. This gives us the first great purpose of our lives, which is to hear God speaking to us on Earth.

Purpose one: hearing God calling us into his love

At one point in my life, I found myself embarking on a new ministry venture for which I felt unqualified. I remember saying to God that I had never done anything like this before and was worried. God simply said back to me, "I have." God's reply made me think about the millions of Christians who he has already walked with to see his purpose for their lives unfold. The idea of walking into this unknown ministry arrangement with such an experienced partner calmed me. I share this story to make the point that our God speaks. The gods of all other world religions don't speak. They communicate through indirect means—never showing themselves. Only the Christian God personally reveals himself and speaks to humanity in Jesus. What is even more amazing is that he continues to speak to us today through the Bible and the Holy Spirit who indwells us (John 16:13). The person who hears the Word of God through the Bible and then does the Word of God by the power of the Spirit[26] is the good soil Jesus talks about (Mark 4:20).

We can become complacent with the incredible fact that God speaks to us, or we can learn to value the amazing truth that, like Moses at the burning bush God is calling to us. The Bible tells us that from his throne of unimaginable glory, God calls to YOU. And the primary thing God is calling you to hear is that he loves you. When this truth takes hold, even just one percent in your life, change begins. The God who called all creation into existence calls to you!

Purpose two: learning to call on God

If the idea that God calls to us is amazing, equally incredible is the idea that we are invited to call on God. Three of the greatest theological movements

[26] Romans 8:13, Galatians 5:16-25, Philippians 2:13, Hebrews 8:10, 10:15-16.

in the history of Christianity all presented the idea that calling on God in "prayer is the chief exercise of the Christian life by which we receive all our daily benefits."[27]

Throughout history, many great Christian leaders have looked to David's statement "*call on me in the day of trouble; I will deliver you, and you will honor me*", as an example of how we should live our lives (Psalm 50:15). When we call on God in prayer, we declare our dependence upon him and then find out how willing he is to act on our behalf (Isaiah 64:4).

God calling to us and us calling back to him is central to our Christian walk (Acts 9:14b). What I mean here is that when we hear God's call to us, and then respond by calling back to him, a relationship between God and us is established. We discussed on day two how this relationship is best understood through a loving Father-to-child dynamic and this teaches us that we are to call on God's mighty love for us. This presents the Christian walk as one lived amid God's love for us. We first learn to hear God's loving call to us and then we learn to call on his love to change us.[28]

When this twofold process of being called by God and then calling on God is established, we experience the Christian walk as it should be.

Purpose three: calling others into God's love

For many years I served as an instructor for the Christian Life and Witness Course that the Billy Graham Evangelistic Association uses to train Christians in preparation for evangelistic outreaches. A key part of this

[27] John Calvin, *Institutes*, book 3, see chapters 1–2, 20. Augustine and Barth say the same thing, Augustine, *On The Trinity*, book 15, chapter 28, section 51. Barth, *The Christian Life*, 43. Also see, Luther, *Large Catechism, Of Prayer: The Lord's Prayer.*

[28] Augustine discusses the idea of the Trinity as a divine community of love and then how the Holy Spirit comes to enable us to live in this loving community on Earth. This is a foundational Christian theological teaching. See Augustine, *On The Trinity*, book 15, chapter 19, section 37; chapter 27, section 50; chapter 28, section 51.

course is called "Operation Andrew", which teaches Christians to be like the Apostle Andrew.

After discovering Jesus, the Bible says the first thing Andrew did was find his brother Peter and bring him to Jesus (John 1:40-42). The remarkable thing to notice here is that Jesus called Peter through Andrew. This shows us that Jesus chooses to use us to accomplish his purpose in the world. Paul speaks about this by telling us that we are *"Christ's ambassadors, as though God were making his appeal through us"* (2 Corinthians 5:20).

It's worth noting that Andrew simply used his ordinary life to bring people to Jesus. Eugene Peterson captures this when he paraphrases Paul, "*So here's what I want you to do, God helping you: Take your everyday, ordinary life—your sleeping, eating, going-to-work, and walking-around life—and place it before God as an offering*" (Romans 12:1, MSG). Christians spend so much time trying to figure out what God's will for their life is, and they forget to find out what God's overall will is, which is <u>to know and show Christ</u>.

When we hear God's call, we experience his loving attention. When we call to God we experience his loving intervention. When we call others to Jesus we partake in his loving mission.

God is more interested in how you serve him, as opposed to where you serve him. As is often said, "bloom where you're planted." If God wants to use you mightily, he knows where to find you.

Purpose four: being used for an eternal purpose

Yesterday we learnt that to know our life's purpose we merge our God-given talents and passions with the Great Commission. This simple idea communicates something important to us, which is that God seeks to elevate our lives from having a temporary purpose to having an eternal purpose. We see this when the Apostle Paul says that we will receive a reward in Heaven if "*what has been built survives*" (1 Corinthians 3:14). Paul is telling us that when we accept Jesus' invitation to walk with him, our normal everyday lives begin to bear eternal fruit (John 15:16). When our lives become about knowing and showing Christ, our ordinary everyday lives take up an extraordinary eternal purpose.

Good soil bears much fruit

If we return to the Parable of the Sower, we now see that our lives become good soil when we live in relationship with God and then live to bring others into relationship with God. Our relationship consists of hearing God's call and then accepting God's invitation to call on him. Our mission involves calling others to come to meet Jesus, specifically his death and resurrection for their salvation. As we know God's love and show God's love we join Jesus and live for the purpose of his Father (John 12:49-50).

Many Christians are trying to live for God without living with God. When we hear God calling to us and call to him in return we are walking in rich relationship with him. Through this simple daily act, God can use our lives to call others to himself, ensuring we "*bear much fruit*" in this life and the next (John 15:8).

Application

Scripture: *"Fear not, for I have redeemed you; I have called you by name, you are mine."* Isaiah 43:1b, ESV

Key thought: God speaks, God listens, and God acts.

Action: Meditate on the truth that God has called YOU by name. Call back to him in prayer about the areas of your life that trouble you, and on behalf of others who don't know Jesus. (1 Thessalonians 5:24).

PART TWO

Walking free from our past and pain

"My chains fell off, my heart was free, I rose, went forth, and followed Thee."

— *And Can It Be That I Should Gain*, Charles Wesley

DAY 8

Walking away from partial obedience

This 21-day journey is structured around the four steps we see when Jesus called Peter. The first step was about understanding Jesus' invitation to walk with God: Father, Son and Spirit, which itself involves the invitation to walk with Jesus into the death of the old and the resurrection of new life and purpose. Now that we have looked at these foundational truths, we can go deeper into what it means to walk away from our past and pain.

Today we will look at obedience, the next day holiness, and then at comparison. This will be followed by two days of understanding God's purpose in allowing pain.

The master key of the Christian walk

In the Christian walk we are changed by God's love. It is God's mighty redemptive love that compels us out of the past and into a new purpose with him (2 Corinthians 5:14). Jesus teaches that his love for us is not seen through the ways the world shows love. God's love for us, and our love for God, is shown through obedience; an obedience that is characterised by trust and love.[29] This simple truth makes obedience what the French call the *passe-partout* for the Christian life, which in English simply means "master key." Obeying God is the master key to walking with God.

The first thing we need to understand about obedience is that it is directly linked to the idea of abiding in Christ (John 15:10). Abiding in Jesus and obeying Jesus are "two sides of the same coin" The Apostle John taught that "*if anyone obeys his* [Jesus'] *word, love for God is truly made complete in them*" (1 John 2:5). This means that we can use obedience as a way of measuring our progress in the Christian walk. If we are actively obeying God, we are abiding in Christ and walking with God, likewise, if we are abiding in Christ through his Word and prayer, we will be empowered to obey.[30]

At this point we have a choice to make: we can get distracted by clever and witty theological thoughts on what it means to obey, or we can simply obey God. In the modern Western world, obedience is often linked with our intentions and not our actions. It is no secret that this mindset has entered the Church, resulting in many Christians who have heard about obedience, can talk about obedience, and even preach about obedience, but who are not practicing obedience. Today, we will look at both this counterfeit partial obedience and then authentic biblical obedience.

Counterfeit obedience

James tells us that if we only listen to and hear the commands of Jesus, we are deceiving ourselves. He goes on to simply say that the right way to walk, is to "*Do what it* [the Bible] *says*" (James 1:22).

---

[29] John 14:15-24, John 15:5-17, Acts 5:32, Philippians 2:8, 1 John 2:3-6.

[30] Philippians 2:13, Hebrews 8:10; 10:5-7, 15-16.

In one of Jesus' parables, Abraham says to the rich man that there is a "*great chasm*" separating him and the beggar Lazarus (Luke 16:26). In the same way, there is a great chasm between those who hear the Word and those who do the Word. The modern Western Church has many strengths, but it also has weaknesses. Perhaps the chief weakness is our tendency to think that because we have talked about the commands of God at Bible study, we have kept them. Friend, just talking is a counterfeit form of action. As the old saying goes "talk is cheap."

We must "adult" for a moment here and honestly assess if our obedience to God is talk-heavy and action-light. Most Christians are educated in how to live the Christian life far beyond their level of obedience. If we want to "*live as Jesus did*" we need to do as he did (1 John 2:3-6).

To illustrate this, consider for a moment the Father, Son, and Spirit having a conversation in Heaven about us. Imagine that they held a conference to talk about our sinful state and they all acknowledged we needed saving. Now imagine they wrote up meeting minutes and even posted on the heavenly equivalent of Instagram and TikTok about the resolution they agreed upon. Can I ask, do you feel that in this scenario they have acted? The truth is yes and no. They have taken a form of action because they have spent a lot of time, money, and angel-power in organising the conference! But we can all see that there is a big "NO" coming, as their action, their doing, or their obedience hasn't involved any real-world activity. Thankfully Jesus did act, entering the world, living purely, dying wholly, and rising completely. Friend, I am sure you can see the point being made here, which is that obedience involves *doing* the commands of God.

Biblical obedience

If what we have heard about Jesus has not radically changed our everyday life, then we have not understood biblical obedience. Biblical obedience begins with what we are looking at, it then moves to what we believe and how we react to what we believe, and then finally to what we do. This gives us four key steps to learning to obey God: looking, believing, reacting, and acting.

Looking and believing

Each morning we have a choice to either open the inner reaches of our minds to the Word of God, or to the things of the world. The first few moments of each day are a delicate time where our inner thoughts are more accessible to us. What we pour into our minds at this point in the day is critical to setting our mental outlook. If we begin our day by pouring social media or even the world's news into our minds, we are allowing these things intimate, unregulated access to our conscious and even our unconscious thought-life. If we, however, obey the Bible and pour the Word of God into our minds, God's eternal truth is the first thing that intimately touches our minds each day.

Later in this 21-day journey we will learn from Jesus through John 3 and Charles Spurgeon that belief and faith arise from what we look at. For now, I want us to understand that what we look at each day determines what we believe and then how we act (James 1:25).

You will not have to attend a Bible-believing Church for very long until someone encourages you to read your Bible and pray each morning. The Lord has been commanding his people to begin each day with his Word for thousands of years. One of the earliest times we see this is God's instruction to Joshua, "*Keep this Book of the Law always on your lips; meditate on it day and night, so that you may be careful to do everything written in it. Then you will be prosperous and successful*" (Joshua 1:8). Perhaps more than any other thing, we see Jesus implement this lifestyle, with him constantly withdrawing to spend quiet-time with his Father. The Scriptures and the life of Jesus remind us that what we fill our minds with forms us—"*For as he thinks within himself, so he is*" (Proverbs 23:7, NASB).

Reacting and acting

Many years ago my mother attended a women's night at our local Church. The speaker for this night pulled out suddenly, so at the last minute, one of the ladies improvised by sharing a few recipes that could help make home life run smoother. On this night my mother wrote down a tuna casserole recipe that we then ate for many years. One day when my mother was sick with cancer, I made this recipe. My mother told me where the recipe was written down and what to do, but because I was a 30-year-old Australian male I, of course, didn't need to read the recipe or do as I was told! I instead made the casserole from memory. The second I put it in my mouth I could tell something was wrong. When my mother ate it, she immediately said to me, "you forgot to put the onion in, the onion gives it all its flavour." You see, the problem wasn't the recipe—it worked— the problem was that I didn't follow it correctly and the result was a tasteless casserole, and a "Maccas run."

The Christian walk works, but the problem is that most of us aren't systematically reading the Bible daily, so we aren't clear on what Jesus commands. And if we aren't clear on the commands of Jesus, we can't follow them.

The process of filling our minds with the Word of God is how we abide in Jesus and his love, and when we don't do this Jesus taught that powerlessness and fruitlessness will follow (John 15:4). If we, however, allow God intimate access to our mind each day, the Bible says that the outcome of this will be a life of holiness, power and fruitfulness.

We must also understand that we don't transform our minds by only listening to and hearing the commands of Jesus Christ, but rather, by walking in the commands of Jesus Christ—by doing them. The chief command of Jesus is to love God, which we do by allowing him to live in us, through us living in his Word.

Jesus intentionally joins abiding and obeying together. The reason for this is that God's love enables us to obey, and obeying lets us know we are abiding in God's love.[31] If we obey out of obligation, our obedience will have no longevity. But if we obey out of gratitude because God's love is known to us, our obedience will last a lifetime.

Change always involves a choice, and the choice we are presented with today is to walk away from our past by choosing to build our lives on the Word of God.

If we do the will of God in the morning, we will find it much easier to do the will of God throughout the day.

Application

Scripture: "*If you remain in me and I in you, you will bear much fruit*" John 15:5

Key thought: Jesus didn't suggest we live in his Word, he commanded it.

Action: Take steps to make your obedience to God talk-light and action-heavy. List some ways you can focus on abiding in Jesus better. Some examples are consistent Scripture reading, calling on God in prayer, Christian fellowship, and service.

---

[31] John 14:15-24, John 15:5-17, 1 John 2:3-6, 2 John 6.

DAY 9

Walking away from unholy holiness

A few years ago, I worked with the Billy Graham Evangelistic Association on a large-scale outreach in Australia. While we were preparing the stadium for the Sydney meeting, I had a rather odd experience.

One of the team members had invited a visiting pastor from India to come for the day to help us set up. In one of the breaks, I got talking to this man about the nature of the Christian walk. This pastor served in the slums of one of India's major cities, which meant he was from a very different world to me. As the conversation progressed, I asked this pastor how he understood the Holy Spirit's role in our Christian walk, and I will never forget the simple answer he gave me.

We had just eaten lunch in a food court, and the pastor drew on this simple experience to say that the Christian walk is just like a food court. He said, "In the Christian walk, we have all sorts of options on what we can choose each day, and the Holy Spirit asks us to choose the right things—things which align with the Bible's teaching. If we say yes, we move forward; if we say no, we move backwards." The Christian walk is simply a matter of what we choose each day, and we need to realise that we have the ability and responsibility to choose wisely (Ephesians 5:15).

This simple story surfaces a deep theological truth, which is that God gives us the ability to choose whether we will walk with him or not. After this conversation took place, I completed a doctoral degree in the doctrine of election. As someone who has advanced training in this area of theology, I want to assure you that what this pastor from India said is 100 percent true. We must choose to walk with Jesus each day, and our daily decisions determine if we walk with God or walk away from God.[32]

Elevating the ordinary

I want to be honest with you, when the pastor from India shared that we need to choose to obey the Holy Spirit in all daily decisions, I heard it, but I didn't do it. While I was obeying God in the big areas of my life, this general obedience had not filtered down into all my daily life choices. I said yesterday that many Christians are educated beyond their level of obedience. Kindly and with love, it is a dangerous thing to meditate on the Word of God each day but not implement it in our daily decisions. The Bible says about this, "*Do not merely listen to the word, and so deceive yourselves. Do what it says*" (James 1:22).

God wants to grow his Church, and he even commands us to bear fruit for his name (John 15:8). When the Bible talks about building the Church, it is not talking about a physical building, it is talking about the life of Jesus entering us and changing our way of walking. Basically, the Church grows when the Christians in it learn to choose Jesus' way of living in the decisions of everyday life. This teaches us that it is one thing to call Jesus Lord, but another to choose him as Lord!

---

[32] Deuteronomy 30:19, Joshua 24:15, 1 Kings 18:21, Matthew 6:33, Colossians 3:17.

The Apostle Peter said that the Holy Spirit is given to those who obey God (Acts 5:32). The power of the Holy Spirit is linked to our obedience: if we want the Spirit to empower every aspect of our lives, we need to obey him in all areas of our life. This goes to the heart of what the pastor from India taught me, which is that being filled with the Spirit's power is not mysterious or random, it is the direct result of choosing to obey God. As William Booth, founder of The Salvation Army said, "The greatness of a man's power, is the measure of his surrender."

For the rest of today, we will look at a key reason many well-meaning Christians struggle to obey God and therefore miss experiencing God's power in their lives.

Has God really said that?

In the Garden of Eden, Satan asked Eve the question: *Has God said?* Satan's tactic was to undermine God's Word as the source of truth (Genesis 3:1). Once Satan had removed Eve's confidence in God's Word, he could redraw the boundaries of what holiness looked like. This didn't result in Eve thinking that it was ok to sin, but rather, in her thinking that sin was now ok. Sin became reframed in Eve's mind so that she believed that what God called sin was no longer sinful. Satan was able to make unholiness seem holy.

What Satan did here was very clever. He didn't say that Eve should sin, rather he made Eve think that her actions weren't sinful. The world may have changed dramatically, but Satan's tactics in our time are the same as they were in the Garden of Eden.

In many sections of modern Western society things the Bible calls harmful are celebrated as healthy, and the things the Bible calls healthy are seen as unhealthy. We see the negative results of these upside-down standards across our communities, but what Christians often don't realise is that this has influenced our understanding of holiness and obedience in the Christian life.

In the Bible we are called to respond to sin with repentance. However, nowadays Christians often respond to sin by saying it is understandable due to their circumstances. I do not wish to upset anyone, but if we respond to sin by talking about it, as we feel it needs to be understood, as opposed to turning away from it, because we know it is wrong, we are entering an unbiblical and powerless place.

Perhaps the most difficult part of this problem to discuss is when we begin to think that suffering makes it ok for us to maintain sinful habits. The Bible has endless compassion for those who have suffered, but this compassion never results in reduced responsibility for our actions. My father gave me a real-life experience of this. My father held others to a high standard of holiness, but he had an incredible ability to excuse his own behaviour because he felt his suffering in life made it understandable.

The Bible says, "*all have sinned and fall short of the glory of God*" (Romans 3:23). I realise this is hard to accept, but when we begin to think that our circumstances exempt us from certain things the Bible calls sinful, then we have effectively fallen for the same lie as Eve. We may not think sin is ok, but we begin to think our actions aren't sinful, because our circumstances make them "understandable." If we seek to "understand" our sin, as opposed to repent of it, we are entering into a conversation or relationship with our sin, as opposed to a relationship with Jesus (Matthew 6:24a).

Sometimes people feel that understanding sin as opposed to repenting of it results in a more kind and loving Christian message. Friend, reducing our responsibility for sin is not kind and loving, it is in all truthfulness the opposite of this, it is oppressive. The reason for this, and the reason I have raised this today, is that if we don't accept sin as sinful, we will never repent of it and never be free from it. Only when we turn from sin are we freed from sin and its consequences (Mathew, 5:29; Hebrews 12: 4-12).

Walking in holiness

My young children often get our dog's leash of the bench, put it on him and pretend to take him for a walk. It is interesting that when our kids pick up the leash and put it on the dog, he never gets excited. Our dog instinctively knows that our kids have no capacity to take him for a real walk, he knows that their offer of a walk is not genuine. In the same way, God knows when our obedience is not genuine. Friend, God blesses genuine obedience, not our version of what we think obedience should look like (1 John 2:4-6).

The Bible says, "*to obey is better than sacrifice*" (1 Samuel 15:22), and Dietrich Bonhoffer said, "one act of obedience is better than 100 sermons." God knows when we are trying to "trick" him by obeying him on our own terms. For many years I was obeying God on my own terms and wondering why no activity from God followed my, so called, obedience. When we obey God generally but not specifically, and when we adopt a holiness level that is based on the world's standard and not the Bible, we should not be surprised when our lives are unfruitful (John 15:4-5).

The encouraging truth here is that even a life that has been unfruitful for decades can become fruitful if we agree with God about holiness, and our response to his holiness (which is obedience). When we agree with God, we receive from God. And he gives abundantly.

The greatest thing you can do to increase your witness for Christ is to radically change a longstanding area of disobedience into an area of obedience. Surrendering past areas of disobedience can become a great gift you can give to the Church. These things can go from being a blockage to a blessing, from a problem to a propellant. All you have to do to move out of barrenness into blessing is choose what Jesus would choose in the "food court of life."

Today, make new choices, surprise those who know you best with obedience to God in the ordinary decisions of life. Where you honked bad drivers, begin to pray for them. When bad things come on the TV, calmly change the channel. When the option comes to overeat, practice restraint. You will find that people's respect for you and interest in your witness for Jesus will skyrocket as you implement obedience in the ordinary.

Application

Scripture: "*Then your Father, who sees what is done in secret, will reward you.*" Matthew 6:6b

Key thought: Our private decisions determine our public impact.

Action: Choose today to make the Bible your standard for right and wrong. Then ask the Holy Spirit in prayer what areas of your life conflict with the Bible. Choose to obey God in these areas, remembering that holiness is simply consistent obedience.

DAY 10

Walking away from unhealthy comparison

We began this 21-day journey with God's command to Abraham, "*I am God Almighty; walk before me, and be blameless*" (Genesis 17:1). If God told Abraham to walk before him, it stands to reason that Abraham had been walking before other things and that God wanted his sole attention. In one sense, nothing has changed since God said this to Abraham. Today, just like in Abraham's age, we have countless other things that are calling for us to walk before them. A common way to describe this is through the concept of "comparison."

The word comparison highlights how we gain our sense of need and worth from things outside of us. The people and places we look to determine so much of how we live. If we look to God to indicate our needs and worth, our life will take on an eternal and sacrificial nature. If we, however, look to the world to tell us these things, our life will be materialistic and focused on the temporary and passing things of this life. What we look to, we walk before. And what we walk before determines what we think we need and who we become (Psalm 1). Today we will contrast three unhealthy things people walk before with Jesus' command to get identity and purpose from following him.

Living in comparison to the world

If God calls us to draw identity and purpose from him, our culture pulls us in a very different direction. So much of the modern world is based around comparing our lives to others. Social media, entertainment, business, and countless other aspects of our world are constantly trying to make us compare ourselves against their chosen standard, hoping we will see a gap in our lives that they can uniquely fill. A key example of this is social media.

Social media is a highly programmed system designed to have us yield our will to the influence of "the algorithm." When I first started my doctorate, I deleted Instagram to focus. I noticed that after a week Instagram began to fret. It started emailing me and seeking me through notifications on my desktop. Instagram was worried it had lost its influence over me.

Social media can be fun and harmless, it can even be helpful for sharing the Gospel, but it can also be a way Satan gets us to move from living under the influence of God, to living under the influence of man. If we live before our social media feed, our identity will be made up of countless micro causes that are all in conflict with each other. When we live for God, we are anchored in one eternal and unmovable cause, which is the glory of God being shown through our lives (1 Corinthians 10:31).

Living in comparison to others

When I was a young pastor I remember following another more established leader on Instagram. I distinctly remember this leader would frequently put up posts where they had large crowds at their house for meals and fellowship.

Almost like clockwork, a few hours after the gathering they would put up a post showing a pristine house, beautifully cleaned as if no one had ever been there. I would see these posts and compare my own capacity against this person and feel terrible. It was only some years later that I found out this leader had several paid staff do the cooking and cleaning for all the functions at their house. These staff were never put on Instagram!

I came to realise that I was comparing my real-life situation with someone else's social media projection. Social media can be a powerful tool for good but it can also be destructive. The lesson here is that we should not compare ourselves against people who we have connection with, but no community with.

Jesus is perfect, but we are not. Even Church leaders can fall into the trap of projecting an image of what they want to be, as opposed to who they are. When we compare ourselves to others as I did, we are drawn away from our unique calling and begin to believe we are being ineffective. Having a thought like this seeded in our mind is deadly to our impact. This is because unbelief is the breeding ground of disobedience and disobedience equals powerlessness. Be inspired and educated by others, but walk before Jesus (1 Corinthians 11:1).

Living in comparison to our upbringing

Growing up we had two palm trees in our backyard. What is interesting about these palms is that their roots don't go down deep like many native trees do in Australia. The roots of palm trees grow in an intertwined pattern, which means they are held in the ground not in their own strength but through the community in which they live. Another way to say that is these trees are held in the ground by what they are living in comparison to. This illustration tells us something about what we choose to live alongside. If we choose to walk with God and live for God, our lives are intertwined with the very thing we were created to be and do. This gives us stability, peace, and purpose in our life. We have already talked about what happens when we intertwine our life with the world and comparison to others, but I wonder how often we consider our relationship with our family.

When we dig down deep enough, we often find that personal, pastoral, and psychological issues in adult life have their roots in experiences we had in our family of origin—the family we grew up in. Like palm trees, our lives develop intertwined with others. If our families are healthy, it will go a long way to helping us be healthy. However, if our family is unhealthy, it means our identity, outlook, and inner self-talk is developed intertwined with unhealthy influences.

Many adults spend their lives trying to earn love and acceptance because they grew up feeling unloved and unacceptable. If this resonates with you, remember that while Satan may have sought to use circumstances to harm you, God has been intertwining his purpose with your life's circumstances to use your experiences for a good purpose (Genesis 50:20).

Most of us have lived our lives so intently focused on issues from our family of origin that we haven't noticed God's activity in our lives. Friend, God has been there all along, gently manoeuvring our life's circumstances to lead us into walking before him.

Living in comparison to Jesus

One Christmas my little children asked Santa for a cubby house. I spent Christmas Eve assembling this cubby house in secret, and then had to lift it in place late at night after the kids had gone to sleep. I attempted to do this lifting by myself and ended up dropping the cubby house and damaging it. A few weeks after Christmas, my five-year-old said to me, "Daddy, Santa's elves didn't do a very good job making the cubby house." My little child was confused why the benevolent "Santa" would deliver her a shabby cubby house.

Many of us feel the same way about God. We wonder why God didn't organise a better family for us to grow up in, or why he put us in this world, especially one containing hypocritical Christians and worldly desires which are constantly pulling at us. Perhaps even more than these points, we wonder where God is when life hurts us most. C. S. Lewis once said that the characters in Shakespeare's plays would never know about the playwright unless he chose to write himself into the story. Friend, God has written himself into your story through your life's unique circumstances, and he has allowed pain and frustration for the good purpose of awakening us to the value of walking with him (Romans 8:28).

Just as God asked Abraham to walk before him, Jesus asked Peter to "follow" him. It is interesting that nearly 2000 years after Jesus said this, social media asks us to "follow" people. I feel this "follow button" makes us devalue the idea of following someone. How often do we click that button without thinking about it? Today, let's do a "following census." Let's place high value on ourselves by only following those who help us grow up into Christ (Matthew 4:19a).

When Jesus called Peter, he could have rejected the offer for any number of personal reasons. Peter, however, was able to understand that the invitation wasn't so much about him as the potential follower, but about the one calling to be followed. What we follow, we compare ourselves to, and what we compare ourselves to, controls us. The truth is that this all boils down to one word, "worship." What we choose to live in comparison to we are worshipping (Exodus 20:4-5a). Worship God. Live your life before God and live in comparison to the value the death of Jesus places on your life. You are so valuable that God died for you (Romans 5:7-8). As the old saying goes:

"I asked Jesus, 'How much do you love me?' 'This much,' he answered, and he stretched out his arms and died." Anonymous.

Application

Scripture: "*The mind governed by the flesh is death, but the mind governed by the Spirit is life and peace.*"
Romans 8:6

Key thought: What you follow forms you.

Action: Today, go through your social media "following" list and "unfollow" things that pull you away from Christ.

DAY 11

Walking with a God who allows pain

"*The thief comes only to steal and kill and destroy. I came that they may have life and have it above the common.*" (John 10:10).[33]

Invited to turn pain into purpose

In the late 1800s a man sat in his office in downtown Chicago. He was a rich and successful lawyer, but a burden began to grow in his heart. This man became concerned that all his time was consumed with his legal profession, and little was left for the Lord's work. After prayer and careful consideration, he decided to leave his job as a lawyer to become a real estate entrepreneur. Chicago was rapidly expanding and great wealth was to be made in buying up land on the city's edges and developing it. Just

[33] Young's translation. Cited in Henry Frost, *Uncommon Christians*, page 3.

as things seemed to be going well, disaster struck in the form of the Great Chicago Fire. This fire levelled the entire city and no one had money or willpower to develop the outlying lands any longer.

After losing everything, this man farewelled his wife and four small children at the Chicago dock as they sailed for Europe in hope of a better life. The man, however, stayed behind to wrap up some business before boarding the next boat. Sadly, the man was never to see his children again. During the trip their boat was struck by another ship and all his children drowned. He learned about it from a telegram his wife sent back to him, which simply read "Saved alone, what shall I do?"

Upon receiving this message, the man boarded another ship to bring his wife back to Chicago. As this ship approached the spot where his children had drowned the captain sent for him, to tell him that they were sailing over his children's watery grave. The man recalled that as they passed over this spot, the words, "It is well with my soul", came into his heart and the mighty Christian hymn that has touched billions of lives was birthed into the world.

This man's name was Horatio Spafford, and due to his faithfulness to the Lord during tragedy, generations of Christians have been comforted, helped, and healed through the mighty Christian anthem that arose from the ashes of his grief.

Walking through pain

After these events, Horatio Spafford had two more daughters and a son. His son also died, this time from sickness. This final tragedy caused Horatio and his wife Anne to take their remaining two daughters and move to Jerusalem to begin a new life. The Spafford family's new life in Jerusalem reminds us about the events of Easter which took place in that same city 2000 years ago. At the heart of Christianity lies the promise of Easter, which is that death gives way to life, and that our deepest scars can produce our most beautiful blessings.

The Easter story begins on Good Friday and then moves to Easter Sunday. What is often forgotten, however, is Easter Saturday, which sits between Jesus' death and resurrection. So many Christians live in-between the death of the old and the embrace of the new. Like Jesus, we are meant to move through painful events towards God's purpose for allowing it, which is new life (Philippians 2:5-13). One thing that stands out from Horatio Spafford's life is that he kept moving through pain, he didn't lie down and declare defeat.[34]

Horatio Spafford's life and the events of Easter teach us two key things. Firstly, that pain is allowed by God for a good purpose, even if we cannot easily comprehend that purpose. Secondly, that we are meant to walk through pain towards the purpose it was allowed for; we are not to stop and make our bed in the painful situation. Today we will look at how we can move through suffering, using pain to propel us into a new life of purpose.

Pain is painful

I believe that we need to pause to acknowledge that pain is painful. Christians can often feel like they are being told to "trust God" and move on. One of Horatio Spafford's remaining daughters, Bertha, saw this in her mother. She recalled in her memoir an incident where a kind person gave her a corduroy coat to combat the cold as a small girl in Jerusalem—as her parents were very poor. She could see the pain in her mother's eyes whenever she wore the coat, and she recalls the reason why:

[34] Spafford was friends with evangelist D. L. Moody, who encouraged him to stay busy and keep moving.

> "As Mother was pulled down [into the ocean as the ship sunk] she felt her baby torn violently from her arms, She reached out through the water and caught Tanetta's little gown. For a moment she held her again, then the cloth wrenched from her hand. She reached out again and touched a man's leg in corduroy trousers."[35]

This story reminds us about the longevity of pain and that hardship is a very real thing. Scripture tells us, "*He will wipe every tear from their eyes. There will be no more death' or mourning or crying or pain, for the old order of things has passed away*" (Revelation 21:4). This is the promise of Heaven and it is a real and true hope, but until we are there we need to learn to live with pain and to extract purpose from it. This purpose will not make the pain go away completely, but it will give us another focus and a reason to keep moving forward in life.

In my mother's well-worn copy of Rick Warren's *The Purpose Driven Life* she wrote the word "ANSWER!" next to the statement, "The very experiences that you have resented or regretted most in life [...] are the experiences God wants to use to help others. They *are* your ministry!"[36] Like Horatio Spafford, my mother suffered greatly in life but chose to walk with God through hardship and testified to God's ability to use her hardest moments to help others the most.

Friend, I don't know your situation, but God does, and he wants you to know that he understands you are hurting. In time, and as you walk with Jesus through this situation, God will do two things. First, he will quiet the pain and make it subservient to joy. This doesn't mean it won't hurt anymore, but rather the pain will lose its ability to hurt you. Second,

---

35 Bertha Spafford, *Our Jerusalem*, page 33.

36 Rick Warren, *The Purpose Driven Life*, page 247.

God will bring a purpose out of your pain, and the experiences that have harmed you will be used by God to heal many. This is God's promise to you (Romans 8:28).

God allows pain for a purpose

The story behind the declaration "it is well with my soul" teaches us that suffering is the nursery of new things. The banksia tree is native to Australia, and it has large seed pods that are programmed to release their seeds in response to the heat that comes from intense fire. By releasing its seeds after a fire, the banksia tree ensures its seeds are dropped into the nutrient-rich soil that occurs after the ash and debris from the fire settles into the ground. This is a picture of how God works in our lives. Through painful situations, God makes us realise the ability we have to seed new life for others.

Fertiliser is an unpleasant substance that can cause great growth, and suffering is the fertiliser of life. If fertiliser is applied wrong it burns the plant it seeks to grow, destroying it. However, when fertiliser is applied by the Master Gardener it causes great growth to occur (John 15:1-12). The same is true of pain, if we try to walk through it without God's help it may well destroy our lives. When we, however, put our future in God's hands, Jesus takes over and makes our unpleasant pain fertilise our life's purpose (Job 42:12-16). Which reminds us of the great hope that awaits all God's children:

> *"He will wipe away every tear from our eyes, and death shall be no more, neither shall there be mourning, nor crying, nor pain anymore, for the former things have passed away."*
> [Revelation 21:4, paraphrased]

Billy Graham's mentor, Raymond Edman, once said, "Never forget in the darkness what God showed you in the light." Friend, pain presents us with a choice: either walk with God through it, or walk away from God because of it. If the Spafford family had walked away from God due to their hardships, we would not be talking about them. The main thing we must grasp today is that *God allows pain for a good purpose.*

There is something powerful about spending a moment determining to stay the course with Jesus and his Church when hardship strikes. The missionary to China, Hudson Taylor, called such people "decided Christians", as opposed to undecided Christians. Today, decide that Jesus and his Word will determine your walk, not your circumstances, however hard they may be.

Application

Scripture: *"For our light and momentary troubles are achieving for us an eternal glory that far outweighs them all. So we fix our eyes not on what is seen, but on what is unseen, since what is seen is temporary, but what is unseen is eternal."* 2 Corinthians 4:17-18

Key thought: God allows pain for a purpose.

Action: I know this can be hard, but choose to believe that in God's hands your pain can fertilise a beautiful new future. Try to list some blessings that have come from hardship, and if able, thank God for these.

DAY 12

Walking through pain into a new purpose

Earthly pain and eternal purpose

We are citizens of Heaven, living for a short while on Earth. The Bible promises that when we get home to Heaven we will either get answers to our questions about why hardship happens, or we will get such love and peace that we will no longer wonder why.[37] This promise is real, and we must cherish it. This noted, we also must acknowledge that we can't access Heaven in this way now, and that we must move towards these eternal answers by faith.

Yesterday we looked at the story of the Spafford family. Both Horatio and his wife Anne found great comfort in the eternal promise of salvation. It was this truth that ensured them their kids were not left in the ocean, but rather "Safe as dear lambs in the arms of Jesus."[38] Horatio was assured

[37] Revelation 21:4, 1 Corinthians 13:12.

[38] I adjusted this quote to modernise it. The quote is: "But I do not think of our dear ones there. They are safe, folded, the dear lambs."

that eternity and not the Earth held his children. Anne Spafford also found comfort in the reality of eternity, stating: "Someday I will understand why my children were taken from me." The Apostle Paul touches this point when he writes, "*Now we see things imperfectly, like puzzling reflections in a mirror, but then we will see everything with perfect clarity*" (1 Corinthians 13:12, NLT). Trying to find answers to our pain through the things of this world is like putting a Band-Aid on a broken arm. When we, however, come to realise the reality of eternity, it opens up another way of approaching our problems, offering us answers that are from "*another place*" (John 18:36).

Today we will look at Jesus' most significant teaching on suffering and learn to apply his eternal solutions to our lives.

Pain orientates us heavenward

Jesus healed and helped many people in the New Testament, but when it came to healing his close friend Lazarus Jesus was absent. When Jesus eventually arrived at Lazarus' funeral his conversation with Martha and Mary gives rich insight into his purpose in allowing pain.

When Jesus arrives, Martha acknowledges his power and begins to ask him to bring her brother back. Jesus replies to Martha's request for an earthly miracle with the promise of a heavenly miracle, saying "*The one who believes in me will live, even though they die.*" Further down in the story it is recorded that Jesus was "*deeply moved in spirit and troubled*" due to the plight of humanity (John 11:1-44). As you read through the exchange between Jesus and Lazarus' family, it becomes clear that Jesus looked through this physical hardship and saw the spiritual predicament of his friends, and gently directed them to a deeper truth. This teaches us that Jesus chooses to use times of physical suffering to make us aware of our spiritual sickness, both for our initial salvation and our ongoing sanctification. I realise this may not be what you want to hear, and I imagine that it was not what Martha and Mary wanted to hear either. What we need to realise is that God's goal and ours are often very different. We want our physical pain to end, while Jesus wants our spiritual sickness to be healed, so that we can live abundantly and eternally with him. This does not mean God cannot grant healing to us in this life, but what it does mean is that Jesus uses painful times to cause us to see the reality of this life and the truthfulness of his Kingdom.

Hardship gives rise to our most impactful ministry

One of the most powerful things a Christian can understand is that their suffering can give them authenticity and credibility in the eyes of others. There is something special about meeting someone who has gone through a similar experience to you and found the light on the other side. For example, Horatio and Anne Spafford moved to Jerusalem and started a ministry for destitute children, one that continues to this day.

It is also interesting that when Martha served Jesus and his disciples before the painful events of John 11 she complained about Mary worshipping Jesus. When Mary, however, worshipped Jesus after Lazarus' death and resurrection the Bible simply says that "*Martha served*" (John 12:2). The painful situation Martha went through refocused her life on what mattered most and enabled her to minister to others with a joyous and upright spirit.

The suffering that Lazarus, Martha and Mary went through caused them to understand their friend Jesus on a whole new level. Through this experience they came to know the sacrificial and eternal nature of Jesus' ministry. It was this hard time that caused the knowledge they had about Jesus to move from their head to their hearts, greatly deepening their walk with him.

Augustine said, "God judged it better to bring good out of evil, than not to permit any evil to exist." This thought reminds us that before we ask Jesus to remove our pain, we should ask him what his will is in allowing it. God doesn't allow pain without a purpose. It may be for our salvation, our sanctification, for us to realise the eternal nature of the Christian walk, or for God to open our eyes to a new ministry calling. Once we know God's purpose in allowing pain, we can gain a new perspective and power over it.

Pain and the promised land

Charles Stanley said, "The dark moments of our life will last only so long as is necessary for God to accomplish His purpose in us."[39] This truth teaches us that once we reach agreement with God about his purpose for our pain, the cloud can lift, moving us forward in life. We must remember that moving forward out of pain looks different in each situation. This acknowledged, we can note that there are two main ways God deals with our hurts. One, God removes the painful circumstance, and two, God removes the circumstance's pain.

These two different solutions are at work in the Bible. In the story of Lazarus, God removed the painful circumstance, but in the Apostle Paul's life, God removed the circumstance's pain (2 Corinthians 12:7-10). We can often feel like Martha must have when Jesus delayed coming to their aid, but we must remember the promise of Scripture, which is that God "*acts on behalf of those who wait for him*" (Isaiah 64:4).

Charles Stanley's powerful statement also reminds us that God uses pain to propel us into our promised land. As mentioned yesterday, we often begin to settle in and live in the wilderness of Easter Saturday. The wilderness represents not where we were, and not where we want to be, but

[39] Charles Stanley, *Life Principle Seven.* In Touch Ministries.

rather, it is in-between the old and the new. Like the Israelites, we are not meant to live in the wilderness. God provided manna for the Israelites and he may have also provided for you in your wilderness, but this doesn't mean he wants you to stay in this middle-ground. When we begin to lose belief in the promise of abundant life, which is life lived in God centred joy, God often allows hardship to get us up and walking again.

Due to mistrust in God's intentions, an 11-day journey took the Israelites 40 years. What looked like God being cold and distant, was God never relenting in his promise to bring Israel into the promised land. What looked like God being unfaithful, was actually God being faithful.

The greatest areas of hardship in our lives have the most potential to propel us into our life's purpose. At this point we have a choice: we can continue to petition God to remove the pain, which he may do. Or we can ask God what his purpose is in allowing a painful time in our life. This question is key to understanding if God desires to remove the painful circumstance or the pain from the circumstance.

Once we understand God's reason for allowing hardship and how he seeks to bring us through it, we can come into agreement with him and move from experiencing pain to experiencing the purpose of this pain.

Application

Scripture: *"You intended to harm me, but God intended it for good to accomplish what is now being done, the saving of many lives."* Genesis 50:20. Also, consider reading Hebrews 12:1-13.

Key thought: Earthly pain redirects us towards eternal purpose.

Action: Ask God how your unique hardships enable you to help others. Pick one person who is going through something similar to you that you can pray for or reach out to.

PART THREE

Walking as Jesus walked

"He walks with me and talks with me along life's narrow way."

— He Lives, Alfred Ackley

DAY 13

Walking and believing

So far in this journey we have looked at Jesus' invitation to walk with him, and his invitation to walk free from the burden of our past and pain. Today, we begin looking at how to walk with Jesus. To do this we will spend the next few days "getting the basics right." The reason for this is that if we get the basic aspects of the Christian walk working in our lives, God can then do fruitful and fantastic things through us. These basics are belief, confession, repentance, and faith. Today we will look at belief.

Our beliefs shape us

The Bible teaches that to change we should not focus on our actions, but rather on our beliefs. As we have said already in this journey, the Gospel is a message of change through love. We can now add to this and say that the Gospel changes us through causing us to believe in God's love for us (1 John 4:16). If we believe in God's love for us, his radical eternal embrace changes who we are and how we live in this life. If we seek to change through "trying harder" or "doing better" we will always fail. The reason for this is that the power to change is being generated by us. If we, however, focus on Jesus' command to let him live in and through us, he is the one generating the change. As we will learn today, the foundation of the Christian life is not doing more, it is believing wholly (1 John 5:5).

Hot belief is best, cold better, and warm worst

The children's fairytale *Goldilocks and the Three Bears* tells the story of a little girl searching for perfection. In the story, Goldilocks tries three different bowls of porridge belonging to the three bears. Goldilocks finds that one bowl is "too hot", another "too cold", and the third is "just right." This story has a parallel to Jesus' words in the book of Revelation, where he says that some Christians are "hot", some "cold", and others "lukewarm" (Revelation 3:15-16). It is interesting to note that in the Goldilocks story the warm porridge is seen as perfect, while Jesus indicates that warm Christianity is the worst option.

To make this point, Jesus uses the example of water. Each day we use hot water to make coffee or tea, and to wash our dishes and clothes, and we use cold water for drinking and for numerous other things. Interestingly, we rarely use lukewarm water. Jesus is saying here that just as hot and cold water are useful, hot and cold Christians are useful. However, lukewarm Christians, like lukewarm water, are rarely used for a dynamic purpose.

The reason for cold Christianity being more valuable than lukewarm Christianity is that when we are "cold", we are far closer to getting to the end of ourselves and fully surrendering to God. Most revivals in history were started by Christians who were deathly cold, and due to this became radically surrendered to God.

Spring follows winter, and it is only when we have felt the cold of winter that we will see the blossoms of spring (James 4:9).

If you are feeling spiritually freezing-cold today, then the Bible teaches that you are closer than ever before to a "hot" belief in Jesus. And remember, hot believing produces hot abiding, and hot abiding a hot Christian walk.

A person to walk with, not a system to learn

We cannot arrive at true belief in Jesus by "thinking it through perfectly." When we do this, we begin treating the Christian walk like a computer program. Friend, God is not a system to be understood, he is a person to know, and this means that we grow our belief in him through relationship with him. Jesus tells us how to do this in John 3 through his conversation with Nicodemus.

Nicodemus saw through the fraudulent "hot spiritual claims" of his colleagues and realised the true "cold" state of his spiritual life and the people. This realisation brought on desperation, which in turn made Nicodemus move beyond his denominational tribe to go and talk with a young Rabbi called Jesus. In their conversation, Jesus tells Nicodemus that belief in God is best understood through the events of Numbers 21 where the Israelites needed to look at a serpent on a pole to be saved. In John 3 Jesus effectively says the following:

> "*Then when anyone was bitten by a snake and looked at the bronze snake, they lived.*" "*Just as Moses lifted up the snake in the wilderness, so the Son of Man must be lifted up, that everyone who believes may have eternal life in him.*"[40]

The key concept here is looking. God provided a solution to the Israelites' problem, but they needed to look at it, focus on it. If they looked,

[40] Numbers 21:9; John 3:14-15, emphasis added.

they lived. When we mix this point with Jesus' statement about not being lukewarm, we realise that those who move from cold to hot Christianity are those who look at Jesus. This is nowhere better seen than in the conversion story of the famous British preacher Charles Spurgeon.

Looking and believing

Charles Spurgeon recalls that on a certain Sunday he longed for spiritual answers. Bad weather made it impossible to get to his normal Church, so he went to a humble Methodist chapel near his house. The regular minister wasn't at the service, so a rough, loud layman got up and preached on Isaiah 45:22, "*Look to Me, and be saved, All you ends of the earth*" (NKJV). Spurgeon remembers the preacher saying you don't have to do anything, or have anything, but just look. Spurgeon also remembered the preacher talking straight to him during the message and saying, "Young man, you look miserable, stop looking to yourself and look to Jesus to completely save you." Spurgeon recalls these memorable words from the preacher: "Young man, look to Jesus Christ. Look! Look! Look! You have nothing to do but to look and live." Spurgeon later said of this experience, "I saw at once the way of salvation." C. S. Lewis sums this up well when he writes: "Look [to] yourself, and you will find in the long run only hatred, loneliness, despair, rage, ruin, and decay. But look [to] Christ and you will find Him and with Him everything else thrown in."[41]

Spurgeon's conversion gives us a real-life example of what Jesus told Nicodemus, which is that looking is the genesis (beginning) of believing. If we want to believe God more, we look at Jesus more. Instead of trying harder and doing more—which never works—we simply remain (abide) in God's love through looking to Jesus through the Word. As we do this natu-

[41] C. S. Lewis. *Mere Christianity*, 188.

ral act, God promises his Spirit will work through us to bring supernatural change (John 15:5).

Your role is not to change yourself, it is to look to the "Changer" and believe that through this habitual looking he will work. The problem is that we so often stop believing in this process, which results in us ceasing to abide. And once we are no longer abiding we will cease to operate in God's power. This creates a power-vacuum in our lives and causes us to revert back to "trying harder" to change ourselves, which never works. Belief in God's faithfulness is key, as it keeps us abiding even when we feel and see nothing. It is this perpetual abiding that Jesus works through to radically change us.[42] Our relationship with Jesus changes us.

Friend, looking to Jesus is to have faith in him, and to trust the promises God has made about him, in him, and through him. This faith and trust produce a deeply personal relationship in which God has embraced us with his wide, open, loving arms. That relationship, that embrace, changes us, as we are relational beings.

We must understand this correctly. Our natural act of consistently looking to Jesus daily through his Word is taken by God and multiplied; just as Jesus multiplied the loaves and fishes. As we undertake "ordinary" abiding, God indwells this very human act and uses it to radically change us, which begins by him changing how we think (Romans 12:2, Philippians 2:13).

We must come to understand that what we look at determines what we believe and what we believe determines how we act in the world (Proverbs 3:7). When we look habitually at Jesus, he enters us and us him (John 6:63, 15:5). This changes our mindset, which creates new desires in us.

[42] John 15:5-7; Romans 1:17, 7:24-8:11; Galatians 1:6, 2:16-20, 3:2; Philippians 2:13; Hebrews 10:16; 1 John 5:5 etc.

Looking at God's love

Many dedicated believers think sinful actions are the cause of their failings in the Christian walk, when it's unbelief that is first causing them to stumble. The missionary Hudson Taylor touched on this when he said, "Sins committed appeared but as trifles compared with the sin of unbelief which was their cause."[43] If we want to change our actions, we need to change what we believe, and Jesus teaches that this is done by changing what we look at.

In John 20:27, Thomas moved from an unbelieving to a believing Christian walk through looking closely at Jesus. When we look closely at Jesus through his Word, we too will be changed by him. There is a temptation here to dismiss this idea due to its simplicity. Friend, this is the error of Naaman who was willing to do a great and mighty thing to save himself, but not willing to humbly submit to God's way (2 Kings 5:13-14).

We cannot walk with God if we don't believe him and we come to believe God when we make looking to his love (as seen at the Cross) the central activity in our lives.

The question now comes to us: will we keep on trying to save ourselves through our version of what we think the Christian walk should look like? Or have we finally become "cold" enough to submit to Jesus' way of being changed by walking with him?[44]

---

[43] Hudson Taylor, *Hudson Taylor's Spiritual Secret*, Chapter 14 The Exchanged Life.

[44] John 4:14, 6:34-59, 7:37-39.

Application

Scripture: *"For Christ's love compels us, because we are convinced* [we believe] *that one died for all, and therefore all died. And he died for all, that those who live should no longer live for themselves but for him who died for them and was raised again."* 2 Corinthians 5:14-15

Key thought: Looking is the genesis (beginning) of believing.

Action: What we look at daily determines what we believe and then do. Consider how this realisation should change your daily routine.

DAY 14

Walking in confession

In Romans 10:9, Paul connects our inner beliefs with our outward action of confession. He says, "*if you confess with your mouth that Jesus is Lord and believe in your heart that God raised him from the dead, you will be saved*" (ESV). In this verse Paul shows us that the New Testament idea of confession involves our whole life.

It is important to understand from the outset of today that we verbally confess what we internally believe: confession is essentially our beliefs manifested. If we want to know what we internally believe about God then we simply need to check what we are saying, or confessing, about God. Today, we will look at what it means for our whole life to confess Jesus as Lord!

Wholly confessing Christ's love

One simple definition of confession is that it means to agree with God, and there are two main things we need to agree with God about. First, who Jesus is (Matthew 16:16), and second, what he accomplishes for us (1 Corinthians 15:3-4). These two points are themselves built upon the idea of God's love for us (1 John 4:15-16). This is best seen in John 3:16 where Jesus teaches that God's love is the foundation all Christian teaching is built upon. It makes sense then to begin today by understanding what it means to confess God's love for us.

Jesus said the first and greatest commandment is, "*Love the Lord your God with all your heart and with all your soul and with all your mind*" (Matthew 22:37-38). In this passage Jesus tells us what to confess and how to confess it. We are to confess the love of God, which comes to us in Jesus to save us, and we are to confess this in our whole life. Jesus uses three Greek words here to describe wholly confessing Christ in our lives. The first word is *kardia* which means heart, the second is *psuché* which means soul, and then *dianoia* which means mind. Jesus uses three different words to emphasise the idea that our whole life (our heart, soul, and mind) needs to love God (Romans 12:1). These three words are intentionally overlapping, in the sense that they all describe a similar thing, which is our entire life loving God.[45]

Yesterday we learnt about the relationship between looking and believing. Today we will unpack this by understanding what it means to confess Jesus in our looking and thinking, and how these control our actions.

Confession and looking

When I first began studying at Bible College a retired missionary taught me for the subject "1 and 2 Samuel." I remember well this kind and faithful older man bringing in his "flannelgraph board" (anyone under the age of 30 you can just Google that!). This missionary used the flannelgraph board to tell us the story of David and Bathsheba. As he told us the story, he put a cloud representing sin over David's eyes, he then moved the cloud to his

[45] *Expository Bible Commentary (1984)*, entry for Matthew 22:37-39.

mind, and finally his arms. The point of this simple visual presentation was to illustrate that sin begins with what we allow in our minds, it then moves to our thoughts, and once the thought takes hold it manifests as action. Most Christians try to tackle sin at the action stage, which is hard. What the Bible teaches is that we should cut sin off at the first stage, which is the looking (or listening) stage.

Jesus said, "*The eye is the lamp of the body. If your eyes are healthy, your whole body will be full of light. But if your eyes are unhealthy, your whole body will be full of darkness*" (Matthew 6:22-23a). We live in a sinful world, which means that impure and sinful images will come across our path unsolicited. When this happens we have a choice to make, which is to look or look away. A spiritual mentor once said to me, there is a difference between seeing and looking. Seeing is often unavoidable, looking is a choice. Jesus talked about our eyes being "healthy", healthy eyes are eyes trained to not just look at Jesus through his Word, but also to look away from things that are inconsistent with his Word. It is amazing how much of an impact simply choosing to look away from impure things has on our Christian walk. When we intentionally choose to honour the Lord through what we look at, we are confessing his standard over our mind and life (Job 31:1).

Confession and thinking

In the same way that we can choose to look at or look away from things with our eyes, we can also choose to dwell on things with our mind. Paul says to "*Set your minds on things above, not on earthly things*" (Colossians 3:2). The Greek word translated as "*Set your mind*" is *phroneó*, and it describes the relationship between our mental looking and our physical doing. In this verse, and other places in the New Testament, Paul is telling us that our mind has eyes of its own. We have a set of natural eyes that we can choose to look at things with, but we also have an internal set of eyes that we can dwell on things with. Just as we can look at unholy and holy things with our physical eyes, we can also choose to look at these things in our mind. Basically, we can think about godly things, or ungodly things, the choice is ours. Another aspect of the Greek word *phroneó* is that it relates to the English word diaphragm. The diaphragm is the muscle in the middle of our body that regulates breathing, and in the same way your diaphragm regulates your breathing, your mind acts to regulate your spiritual life.

We don't often think about our thoughts as a form of confession, but in many ways, this is the most powerful form of confession. Jesus said to love God with our entire life through our heart, soul and mind, and these are all internal areas of our body. When we control our thoughts by fixing them on the things of God, our entire life is confessing who God is and what he has done for us.

A set mind controls our actions

The person with a set mind is someone who understands the difference between the process of making a decision and being decided. On day eight we looked at counterfeit obedience, which *talks* about obeying God but doesn't actually obey. A set mind is not talking about or thinking about controlling what it dwells on, but has decided to "*take captive every thought to make it obedient to Christ*" (2 Corinthians 10:5). Satan wants more than anything to trick us into thinking that we don't have a choice; that we are enslaved to sinful thoughts and desires. This is not true. Because Jesus has illuminated our minds, we can choose what we think about (Romans 7:24-25).

Our private thoughts make up our public confession, and if we choose the mind of Christ, we will have the power and peace of Christ in our public life (1 Corinthians 2:16).

The Bible says, "*The heart is deceitful above all things and beyond cure. Who can understand it?*" (Jeremiah 17:9). The Hebrew word translated as "heart" is *leb*, and it means the inner and most cherished desires of our minds—the thing our mind wants more than anything else. Commenting on this A. W. Tozer wrote, "In every Christian's heart there is a cross and a throne, and the Christian is on the throne till he puts himself on the cross. If he refuses the cross he remains on the throne."[46] Your mind is the throne of your life. When we choose to confess in our mind that Jesus is God and that he has freed us from our sinful past, this internal confession changes us (Philippians 4:8-9).

The reason this confession changes us is not because of anything we do. Confessing biblical truth changes us because Jesus' words are living. We see this in John 6:63b where Jesus says, "*The words I have spoken to you—they are full of the Spirit and life.*" There is a mystery here that we may not understand but we can still obey, which is that when we fill our mind with God's word, we are filling our mind with God himself. And where God reigns there is rest.

Decide today that you will confess internally and externally that "*God so loved the world that he gave his one and only Son, that whoever believes in him shall not perish but have eternal life*"(John 3:16).

This simple act of ensuring the Gospel reigns in your mind and speech will have a large impact on who you are.

---

[46] Tozer, *The Radical Cross*, Page 22.

Application

Scripture: *"Carefully guard your thoughts because they are the source of true life. Never tell lies or be deceitful in what you say. Keep looking straight ahead, without turning aside."* Proverbs 4:23-25, CEV

Key thought: What we confess we do.

Action: In your mind confess that Jesus is Lord and that he has saved you from negative and sinful thoughts. Then, confess out loud that Jesus is Lord, and that you will not *look* at the sinful things you *see*.

DAY 15

Walking repentantly

If there is any topic in this 21-day journey that will make you feel heavy, I imagine it will be repentance. Sadly, the word repentance has been misrepresented more than any other idea in the Bible. When we hear the word "repent", we normally associate it with someone telling-us-off over sin, with the outcome of this being a condemnation-induced change in our lifestyle.

The Bible frames repentance not through condemnation, but by God's love and forgiveness (John 3:16-17). Sin is rightfully "condemned" in the Bible to get us to look up and see God's loving offer of salvation (Romans 5:18). It is God's love that powers change in our lives. This is seen in the parable of The Prodigal Son, which we looked at on day two. The father stands at the gate searching for his sinful son, and when he sees him at a distance, he runs to embrace him. That is a picture of God's heart overflowing with forgiveness even before the words of repentance stumble out of our hearts.

Today, we will look at the real biblical idea of repentance, and this starts by understanding the original Greek word Jesus used in the New Testament.

Repentance as it should be

At the start of his ministry Jesus says, *"The kingdom of God has come near. Repent and believe the good news!"* (Mark 1:15). The Greek word that the English Bible translates as repentance is *metanoia. Meta* means after and *noia* is the Greek word for mind, which makes repentance mean "the after-mind" or "forward-understanding."[47] The core idea of repentance is that Jesus causes us to think differently, which in turn makes us act differently. Repentance is all about updating our thinking, to then change our behaviour.

Jesus is telling us in Mark 1:15 that we should move forward in life by believing in the Kingdom of God and living for this heavenly reality. Another important time we see the word *metanoia* used is in Acts 3:19 where Peter says, "*Repent, then, and turn to God, so that your sins may be wiped out, that times of refreshing may come from the Lord.*" In this verse, Peter uses the word *metanoia* in relation to sin, and he is telling us that we move forward by moving away from sin. When we put these verses together, we understand that in the New Testament repentance is a call to move forward in life through moving away from sin by moving towards the Kingdom of Heaven.[48]

If we only think that we need to move away from sin, then repentance becomes mere condemnation, as it's all about sin and it offers nothing new to replace sin. On the other hand, if we make repentance all about the newness of God's Kingdom and never mention sin, it becomes powerless as no change in behaviour is required. When we, however, understand that repentance involves a call away from sin and a call into a new life with

[47] Treadwell Walden, *The Great Meaning of Metanoia*, page 7.

[48] Theologically speaking, repentance always follows faith. John Calvin wrote, repentance "flows from it [faith], or is produced by it as fruit from a tree." John Calvin, *Institutes of the Christian Religion*, book 3, chapter 3, section 1, paraphrased.

God, then the concept is functioning properly, and it becomes freeing. Perhaps the simplest way we can understand repentance is through two words, "leave" and "come." Leave sin and come to abundant life with God.

Now that we understand what repentance means, we can spend the rest of today looking at three key aspects of this powerful command.

Repentance involves leaving sin

On day six Billy Graham reminded us that it is possible to repent without obeying: "We can be convicted of sin—we can pray and confess our sin—we can repent—but the real test is our willingness to obey."[49] This quote reminds us that true repentance involves a change in what we are doing. This leads to the simple truth that repentance involves walking away from sin, through abiding in God's loving embrace (2 John 6).

There are many versions of "truth" operating in our society and even in our Churches in this age. On day nine we considered how some versions of the Gospel that are preached nowadays call for sin to be "understood" instead of forsaken. Friend, I don't want to come across as mean-spirited, but anything other than ceasing to sin is counterfeit repentance. Kindly, and simply, real repentance means to stop sinning habitually (Ephesians 2:1-5, Colossians 3:5).

Repentance involves coming to the Kingdom

Repentance involves accepting that God loves you and wants to be with you eternally. In the book of Revelation, a beautiful picture is painted of the eternal city of God which will descend to Earth in the age to come. This city is in the shape of a cube, it is taller than any building on Earth and made up of enough levels to house billions of people (Revelation 21:9-27).

---

[49] Billy Graham, *The Holy Spirit*, 234.

This city is not a fantasy, it is a biblical reality and our real home. We are called to repent of living from our old identity as a citizen of this broken world, and to adopt a new identity as a citizen and even ambassador of this real eternal city (2 Corinthians 5:16-21).

On day three we looked at the key way we distinguish ourselves as citizens of God's Kingdom, which is through living for God's glory by adopting a sacrificial way of life. God calls us to leave a lifestyle of working for our own personal gain and to come to a way of life that loves God and others above ourselves.

Repentance is made possible by God's love

In Romans 12:2 the statement "*be transformed by the renewing of your mind*" contains the same two Greek words that make up repentance—*meta* (after) and *noia* (mind). It is also interesting that the Greek word for "*transformed*" that Paul uses in Romans 12:2 is the same word used in the Gospels for the transfiguration of Jesus (Matthew 17:2). These points lead to an important truth, which is that repentance is accomplished by God's transfiguring power.

One of the most important things we need to understand about salvation is that it is something God accomplishes in us.[50] It is God's love poured into our hearts which illuminates us to our need for God (Romans 5:5). God's love is the source of our change and the means of our change.[51]

On day four we learnt from the Bible, John Owen, Tim Keller, and John Piper that it is God's love poured into our heart that our Christian walk is built upon. Although we could dive into heavy theology to explore this point, the simple thing we need to understand is that <u>salvation is some-</u>

[50] This is a foundational principle in evangelical, reformed, and spirit filled missionary theology.

[51] Evelyn Christenson, *Lord Change Me*, page 82.

thing God accomplishes in us. Another way to say this is that you don't need to save yourself—your Bible reading and prayer life is about receiving repentance not achieving repentance.

God's love as seen in Jesus Christ is the change agent of the Christian life (2 Corinthians 5:14). Maybe some of us need to ask God to empty us of sin, by filling us with his love.[52]

Unbelief, a key repentance blocker

Many Christians feel like they have repented a million times and still fail to walk in holiness. When we feel this way, it is best to focus on the root cause of our problem, which is unbelief.[53] Many believers are more than willing to acknowledge sin in their life, but are unable to believe that God can use them for a new purpose. Their identity is still in who they have been, not in who they are becoming (2 Corinthians 5:17). The Christian stuck in this place doesn't have a forward-mind—a meta-mind—they have a back-mind or past-mind, which is why they can't move forward into new life with God. Their mind is consumed with their past failings, not their Father's love (John 14:21-23). The New Testament call of *metanoia* (repentance) is a call to have our mind enter upon a new stage of thinking by being filled with the knowledge of God and his Kingdom.[54]

On day thirteen we read the following thought from Hudson Taylor, "Sins committed appeared but as trifles compared with the sin of unbelief which was their cause, which could not, or would not take God at his Word."[55] Many Christians struggle to walk with God richly because they have only heard one half of repentance, which is the command to leave sin.

---

52 John 4:14, 6:34-59, 7:37-39; Romans 5:5.
53 John 16:9, NLT; 2 Peter 1:4-5; 1 John 5:4-5.
54 Treadwell Walden, *The Great Meaning of Metanoia*, page 7.
55 Hudson Taylor, *Hudson Taylor's Spiritual Secret*, Chapter 14 The Exchanged Life.

When we have not joined this command to leave sin with the command to come into the Kingdom, we have nothing new to move forward into. Just as people cannot live without purpose, we cannot repent without believing it will bring new and wonderful things into our life. As the writer to Hebrews says, "*anyone who comes to him must believe that he exists and that he rewards those who earnestly seek him*" (Hebrews 11:6).

Some Christians have been in the same place with God for decades. Today God is calling you into a new journey with him. God is not going to hurt you, he has something beautiful planned for you. Trust him. Today, say yes to God by believing in him and his Kingdom, and as you turn to Jesus' way of walking, "the things of Earth will grow strangely dim in the light of his glory and grace."[56]

Application

Scripture: "*…And the blood of his Son Jesus washes all our sins away.*" 1 John 1:7b, CEV

Key thought: Repentance involves leaving the old life to gain a brand new life.

Action: Today, make a change to your prayer life. Yes, repent of sin, but now ask God to deal with sin in you, for you, by filling you to overflowing with his love. (Romans 5:5).

[56] Helen Lemmel, *Turn Your Eyes Upon Jesus.*

DAY 16

Walking by faith

Today we will look at two key observations about faith from Scripture and then apply these to our lives.

Faith—our foundation

Most Christians get to the point in life where they have tried to live for God in their own strength and found that this doesn't work. Five hundred years ago, a man named Martin Luther came to this place and began searching the Bible for an answer as to why his walk with the Lord was so powerless. The American theologian Donald Bloesch describes this moment well:

> While wrestling with Paul's epistle to the Romans, Martin Luther was suddenly struck by the words from the prophet Habakkuk cited by Paul in Romans 1:17: "*He shall gain life who is justified through faith*" (NEB). It then dawned on Luther that the righteousness of God is not a prize that can be earned by works of love but a gift that enables man

> to do such works.[57] Salvation is not a matter of working one's way into heaven but of being received into the favor of God.[58]

Martin Luther's revelation was that we are not saved by anything we do. We simply put our faith in Jesus for him to apply to our lives what he has already done (Romans 4:4-5). And this same principle is how the Christian walk works. We daily come to God through his Word and ask him in prayer to make us in practice what we already are in status.

There is something powerful about simply believing that you have been made right with God through Jesus Christ (Romans 3:22). Having faith in this one truth changes our identity. It stops us from striving to "be good enough" and it enables us to walk forward in life confident that God is with us and willing to help us.

All other belief systems in the world tell us to "do more", whereas the Christian Gospel tells us to "believe more." When we believe, we will have faith in Christ, and he will move us forward in life, out of the old and into the new.[59]

Faith makes us confident to move forward

Yesterday we learnt that repentance moves us forward in life by moving us away from sin and towards Jesus and his Kingdom. Faith is a critical

57 "*It is Jesus' name and the faith that comes through him.*" Excerpt from Acts 3:16.

58 Donald Bloesch, "The Sword of the Spirit." Language modernised. See Hudson Taylor, "The Exchanged Life" for a real world example of this. See also, John Calvin, *Institutes of the Christian Religion*, book 3, chapter 3, section 1.

59 Jesus Christ is the acting power in faith (Romans 4:4-5). Martin Luther famously said that it is not so much faith, but rather the object of faith that matters, meaning: "Faith looks to Jesus Christ [...] Christian faith is not an inactive quality in the heart. If it is true faith it will surely take Christ for its object." Martin Luther, Commentary on Galatians 2:4-5,16.

part of this process. If we do not have faith in Jesus' willingness to help us in life, we will cease walking with him and our forward progress in life will stop. Faith in Jesus fuels walking with Jesus. Faith keeps us walking with Jesus even when we can't see anything on the horizon or feel him in a situation. The person with faith in Jesus allows the future promise of God to determine their present actions.

Hebrews 11:1 says, "*Now faith is confidence in what we hope for and assurance about what we do not see.*" A simple explanation of this verse is that it encourages us to have faith in faith! The Bible is assuring us that faith works as advertised.

We must have confidence that Jesus will come to the person walking obediently by faith and personally work in their situation for good (Luke 7:9). As Hebrews 11:6 reminds us, "*without faith it is impossible to please God, because anyone who comes to him must believe that he exists and that he rewards those who earnestly seek him.*"

For the rest of today, we will look at how our faith in Jesus helps make our everyday lives fruitful for Jesus.

Having faith for others deepens our faith

The last section of this 21-day journey takes us through Jesus' final invitation to Peter, which is to walk others to himself. Once Peter learned how to walk with Jesus, he was able to then walk others to Jesus. One of the unexpected aspects of beginning to walk others to Jesus is the faith journey it takes us on. As we begin to be burdened by people's need to know Jesus, an awareness grows in us about our own lack of power. Our desire to lead others to Jesus results in the Holy Spirit leading us into a deeper walk with Jesus. The more we love others the more we are pressed into loving God, so that he can shine through us in a powerful way.

The question could be asked at this point about why God seemingly makes it so hard to reach people. Why doesn't God just give us the power immediately to convert others? Taking us on a long personal journey of surrender so that we can be filled with his Spirit and power seems inefficient.

The reason for this is found in John 15:15 where Jesus says that we are his friends and not his servants. The master of a servant has no interest in the servant's personal development, he just wants to use the servant for "tasks." Friends, however, have ownership of each other's lives; they love and care about each other. Jesus treats us as friends and therefore doesn't just use us to do "tasks." Jesus takes us on a faith journey where we are changed into his likeness, and a key way this happens is through us seeking his power to reach others. The truth is that it's normally when we try to reach others for Jesus that we realise how unlike Jesus we are, and it's this awareness that causes us to seek him in a new way.

Jesus or bust

As we seek Jesus in a new way, we will come to understand that Jesus wants us to learn to rely on him above everything else. To do this, Jesus takes us into situations where everything we once trusted in is stripped away. The result of this is a Christian walk totally reliant upon God.

I once heard the preacher Louie Giglio say that when astronauts land on the Moon they come to a point in their descent where they enter what is called "dead man's curve." Dead man's curve is the name given to the point where the astronauts can't return to the orbiting spaceship if something goes wrong. Once the astronauts pass this point, all other options are gone and they must press forward to landing on the Moon, no matter what.[60]

---

[60] Louie Giglio, sermon titled "What is Worship."

God desires for us to have a genuine encounter with his faithfulness in our Christian walk, and the way this happens can be like us having our own "spiritual dead man's curve" experience. It is only when all other options are stripped away that we come to Jesus with a willingness to give him everything. And once we surrender all, Jesus provides all.

A real-life experience of God's faithfulness

God doesn't force us into a place of total reliance upon him, he invites us. Maybe, as you have been walking with the Lord over the past few weeks, he is inviting you to trust him in a great way in an area of your life today. This always involves uncertainty in some way, shape, or form, and it is this uncertainty that God uses to show us how faithful he is.

The need has never been greater for Christians to boldly embrace the uncertainty of a faith journey (of dead man's curve) to build new things for God's Kingdom. I wonder if God is calling you today to step out of the boat, so to speak, and do something new for his glory. Maybe it's talking to a colleague about Jesus? Maybe God wants you to enter a new ministry area? Or maybe God wants you to believe afresh for the salvation of a long-lost loved one? God is always leading us into new experiences so that he can show us his faithfulness in new ways.

Let's put ourselves into situations where we need to have great faith, so that we can experience Jesus' faithfulness greatly. Let's not live for comfort, let's live by faith, trusting that through Jesus the unreachable can be reached and the impossible be made possible (Romans 4:17).

If Peter hadn't stepped out of the boat, he would never have walked on water!

Application

Scripture: *"For in the gospel the righteousness of God is revealed—a righteousness that is by faith from first to last, just as it is written: 'The righteous will live by faith.'"*
Romans 1:17

Key thought: Fear paralyses us, faith moves us forward.

Action: Identify something you can do for God that requires faith. Take steps to do this. Consult a wise Christian about it, if needed.

DAY 17

Walking and the call of God (cockroach soccer)

The call

In Acts 9 we see "Saul" called by Jesus to leave his old life and take up a new one as "Paul." Once he agrees and walks away from his old life, Jesus sends Ananias to Paul to tell him that from now on he is to "*carry*" the name of Jesus (Acts 9:15, ESV). Like Peter, Paul wasn't saved to sit, he was saved to help others be saved.

Paul's experience reminds us that God calls us to two main things. The first is to follow him and the second is to lead others into following him. These two points can be seen through what Jesus called the greatest and second greatest commandments, which are love God and love others (Matthew 22:36-40). The Christian walk is centred around loving God through leading others to him.

So far in this 21-day journey we have looked at Jesus' invitation to walk with him, Jesus' invitation to walk away from our past, and the invitation to walk as Jesus did. The final part of this 21-day journey will be dedicated to looking at what it means to walk in a way that leads others to Jesus. And the first step of this is understanding God's call to us.

God's call to us is rarely logical

When I was 26 years old, I finished my undergraduate studies and student pastor role and began my first paid job as a pastor. I remember wrestling with whether I should take this job as it was in a Church plant in a rough part of Sydney. My friends were all moving into roles in established Churches and I was being led into a very different scenario.

It was at this early point in my life that I had to decide if I was going to obey God's leading or serve him on my own terms. I said yes to God and ended up running a youth group in a government school hall, which was itself located within a government housing estate. The Church was so poor that we didn't have money for any sports equipment, so the kids improvised by inventing "cockroach soccer." The school hall we met in was infested with cockroaches, so there was always an ample supply of roaches in case one got injured in the competitive game. I remember watching the kids the first time they started to use the cockroaches as makeshift soccer balls and thinking that I had really got myself into an interesting situation.

Despite the resource problems in the Church, the ministry was thriving. The youth and young adults' groups grew dramatically, the kids' club exploded, and the leadership teams for these ministries thrived. The environment was unpleasant, but the ministry was having a noticeable impact.

As I came to the end of my first year in this role, our humble Church became involved in the executive leadership of the large evangelistic meeting the New York evangelist Nicky Cruz was holding in Sydney. I had read the book about Nicky Cruz, *The Cross and the Switchblade*, in school for an assessment some years earlier. I don't know what I would have thought if I had known in Mr Warren's year 9 English class that I would end up meeting Nicky Cruz and ministering with him.

While the Nikky Cruz outreach was being organised, the senior pastor's wife passionately recommended a book to me. I have a distinct memory of standing in the pastor's kitchen and his wife handing me the book *Fresh Wind Fresh Fire*, written by another New Yorker, pastor Jim Cymbala of the Brooklyn Tabernacle. Interestingly, a few years earlier I led at a summer camp near New York City with The Salvation Army. Through this experience, I met the Salvation Army coordinators of the September 11 Ground Zero site in New York City and stayed at their home in Long Island. I began to see that God had led me to this unassuming Church plant to expose me to a Gospel centred, faith-filled, and Spirit-empowered version of Christianity from New York City. This experience led me into evangelistic circles in Sydney that resulted in me serving for many years with Billy Graham's family as they held outreaches across Australia, furthering my exposure to rich evangelistic ministry.

All my many years of evangelistic ministry in Sydney trace back to one decision to say "yes" to Jesus' call to serve him in a cockroach-infested school hall. If I had taken the sensible and safe option, none of the relationships and experiences that helped form me would have happened. God called me to take a step of faith into a seemingly unreasonable experience because he knew it would lead to extraordinary experiences.

God calls to us "leave"

The above story illustrates how God works in our lives. God calls us out of the old and into his new plan for our life. Our version of new life with God normally looks like our old life with slightly better morals, but when we say yes to Jesus' invitation to walk with him, he offers us a radically new life with him.

Peter had to obey Jesus' call to leave fishing for fish to begin fishing for people. Abraham obeyed God's call to move from Ur of the Chaldeans to Canaan (Israel). Paul left his life of prestige in Jerusalem to live a life on the road and on the run. A key thing we notice all throughout the Bible and in Church history is that God is always calling people to leave. God is continually calling his people to leave what they know to discover a new life with him. However, God's call to leave is not a-one-size-fits-all thing. God calls some people to leave places, others he calls to leave habits, some he calls to leave relationships, and some to leave an old mindset. The point here is that God's call to us involves "leaving" (Genesis 12:1).

God calls us to carry his name

Paul is told to "*carry*" the name in Acts 9:15 (ESV). This is an important statement as it tells us that the message of the Gospel is embodied in the name Jesus.[61]

The English name Jesus comes from the Hebrew name *Yeshua*, and *Yeshua* is a word containing two key thoughts. The first is the name of God that was revealed to Moses, which is "YHWH."[62] The second thought is the word "saves." The name of Jesus literally means "YHWH-saves." When the Bible tells us to carry the name, it is telling us to carry the message that God saves through Jesus, otherwise known as the Gospel.

For Paul and us, carrying the message that God saves through Jesus means that we need to cease carrying all other conflicting messages. The call of God is simple, but it is also invasive. God calls us to take up his name, and, in doing so, put down all other ideas that conflict with him, his message, and mission.

---

[61] This is a consistent theme in the first few chapters of Acts.

[62] Yeshua is the oldest known Hebrew name containing the tetragrammaton, which is the four letters YHWH.

God calls us to see something come out of nothing

Every Church in existence was at one point not there. Every Church in our community was believed into existence. At some point in the past, some believers—maybe now long gone—had faith for nothing to become something. Paul mentions this in Romans 4:17 (NLT) when he says, "*Abraham believed in the God who brings the dead back to life and who creates new things out of nothing.*" The Berean Standard Bible translates this verse to say, Abraham believed in "*the God who gives life to the dead and calls into being what does not yet exist.*"

Romans 1:14 says that Abraham "*is our father in the presence of God*" (BSB). Paul is telling us here that the Church is "fathered into existence" or "brought into existence" under the idea that God can make nothing into something for his glory. Basically, bringing something out of nothing is in the DNA of the Church. It is interesting to consider that when God brings something out of nothing missionally in our communities, he is mirroring the original creation story where he brought our universe into being out of nothing. This point is connected to the nature of faith in Hebrews 11:1-3. It is like God is telling us that we only truly understand faith when we take up his offer to mirror the original creation story and see something come out of nothing through our lives, for his glory.

The missionary Lillias Trotter left everything she knew in England to plant a new work for God in Algeria. Upon landing in this foreign land feeling weak and unqualified, Lillias famously said "Truly if God needed weakness, He had it!" The Bible tells us we are qualified to do new things for God when we become weak enough to totally rely on Jesus' power (2 Corinthians 12:10).

God wants to use us

The world now has a population of over eight billion people. This means that never in the history of humanity have the eternal futures of so many people depended on the actions of so few.

Imagine if Jesus hadn't left Heaven, or Peter fishing, and Paul the past. God called them all to "leave", often illogically, and, once they left, God taught them to become weak enough to channel his power. This is the way God builds—he calls us into strange situations so that we are emptied, and then we learn to embrace his love and power. As Hudson Taylor, who left his life in England for a new life in China said: "God chose me because I was weak enough. God does not do His great works by large committees. He trains somebody to be quiet enough, and little enough, and then He uses him."

Application

Scripture: *"God planned for them to be like his Son; and those he planned to be like his Son, he also called; and those he called, he also made right with him; and those he made right, he also glorified."* Romans 8:30, ICB

Key thought: God personally calls to us.

Action: Today, can I encourage you to pause to hear what God is emphasising to you today:

- Is God calling you to leave something?
- Is God calling you to exclusively carry his name?
- Is God calling you to see nothing become something?
- Is God calling you to weakness, to experience his power?

PART FOUR

Walking others to Jesus

"*The first thing Andrew did was to find his brother Simon* [Peter] *and tell him, 'We have found the Messiah' (that is, the Christ). And he brought him to Jesus.*"

John 1:41-42

DAY 18

Walking and the Great Commission

In section one we looked at who God is and how his Gospel operates in our life. In section two we discussed moving past our past and why God allows pain. Section three sought to get the basic ideas of belief, confession, repentance, and faith working in our Christian walk. Now that we have moved through these three areas we come to the final part of our journey, which is learning to walk others to Jesus.

A small word of explanation. This final section isn't designed to present an evangelism and discipleship "system" or "program." These final days are dedicated to looking at some key aspects of inviting others to Jesus in the Bible, which are: the Great Commission, the Church, our motivation and power, and eternity.

The basic purpose of this final section is to grow our understanding of God's mission, so that we can invite others to walk with Jesus in a greater way. As we dwell on these things, let's ask the Holy Spirit to guide us into areas that we need to grow in, so that others can come to know Jesus through us.

Walking others to Jesus

Today, we begin by looking at Jesus' famous words to his disciples just before he went to Heaven:

> "*Go and make disciples of all nations, baptizing them in the name of the Father and of the Son and of the Holy Spirit, and teaching them to obey everything I have commanded you. And surely I am with you always, to the very end of the age*" (Matthew 28: 19-20).

This statement has four simple parts to it. The first is to go, the second is to make disciples, the third is to teach these disciples to obey, and the final one is the assurance that Jesus is with us. To help us walk others to Jesus, we will look at these four points today.

Go

Jesus' command to make disciples of all nations was a radical idea. The first disciples of Jesus had grown up in a religion that was designed largely around keeping others out. The command to "*make disciples of all nations*" was the complete 180-degree opposite of what the original disciples had grown up with. They went from a worldview centred around staying in the Jewish homeland and keeping others out of this land, to going to the Gentiles and inviting them into a relationship with God. Basically, Jesus' final command to his disciples was to no longer "stay" but to "go." The application of this to our modern lives is that we should not wait for people to come to our Churches to share Jesus with them, we should go to them.

I once helped run an evangelistic outreach in Broken Hill in outback Australia. As part of this outreach we organised some activities at the local skatepark to encourage the kids to come and hear the Gospel at the meeting in the evening. A large group of kids from the skatepark came along that night and sat with me as the Gospel was preached. As the evangelist invited people forward to receive Jesus, I distinctly remember these kids getting restless and motioning that they wanted to move. I got worried they were wanting to leave and tried to get them to sit down. At that point one of the boys said to me in true outback English, "Nar sir, we wanna go down the front." I was embarrassed at my lack of faith and inspired by their courage. As they went down the front, a leader at a local Church that was across the road from the skatepark saw them coming and came over to counsel them. Afterwards this Church leader said they had seen these kids in the skatepark for years and just never thought to "go" over the road and talk to them—which they faithfully did after the outreach.

I don't share this story to condemn anyone, but simply to point out that we may need to supplement our next prayer meeting for revival in our community, by "going" out into our community seeking people to revive (Matthew 9:37).

Make disciples

As all parents know, it is one thing to have a child but another thing to raise a child well. This simple thought helps us understand the difference between converting people and making mature disciples.

Paul gives us insight into what the process of making disciples of Jesus looks like in Ephesians 4:12-13. In this passage Paul points to "*unity in the faith and in the knowledge of the Son of God*" as key markers of being a "*mature*" follower of Jesus Christ (Ephesians 4:13). Paul is saying here that we cannot expect someone to live out Christian morality and the Christian mission if they are not first in Christian community and growing in their knowledge of Jesus Christ.

A key part of introducing someone to following Jesus is bringing them into Christian community, or as Paul says "*unity in the faith.*" Once people are in Christian community they can be taught how to walk with God through his Word and prayer, making them mature in their "*knowledge of the Son of God.*" Simply said, we are to introduce people to walking with Jesus through his Word, and this is best done through Christian community—the Church.

Once the person begins to walk with the Lord, their character, conduct and direction in life will change. This is what Jesus did, he built a Christian community and centred that community in following him. Once these two critical things were happening, everything else followed. Getting in Christian community and in the Word are critical to walking with Jesus.

Teach them to obey my commands

Here Jesus instructs us that obedience to his commands is a central part of making disciples. On day eight we looked at what it means to obey the commands of Jesus. We learnt that there is no substitute for obeying God's command to abide in him through remaining in his Word. As we obey this primary command, the Word of God which is "*full of Spirit and life*" will cause Jesus Christ to occupy our lives and enable us to live differently (John 6:63).

Asking people to live the Christian life without Jesus Christ in their hearts is asking the impossible.[63] Paul tells us that anything other than Christ graciously changing us through relationship with him is "*a different gospel*" or "*no gospel at all*" (Galatians 1:6-7). We must be mindful to ensure that our discipleship programs do not present a list of rules to obey, but

---

[63] Philippians 2:13, Hebrews 8:10, 10:16.

rather, instruct people how to walk with Jesus through his Word, so that he can make us like himself (1 John 2:5-6).

I am with you always

Jesus lived, died and rose 2000 years ago. This can make us feel like we are separated from him and at a disadvantage to the original disciples. It is interesting to contrast this thought with Scripture, specifically the idea that when Jesus was with the disciples they were often confused about his message and mission.[64] A significant transition happens in the disciples' minds and hearts after the Holy Spirit comes to them.[65] This transition is foretold by Jesus himself when he says, "*it is for your good that I am going away. Unless I go away, the Advocate* [Spirit] *will not come to you*" (John 16:7).

Before Jesus' ascension and the coming of the Holy Spirit the disciples were constantly faltering and struggling. However, after the events of Acts 2 there is really no mention of the disciples faltering. In fact, they oversaw an incredible expansion of the Church into the world around them while under intense persecution. The point here is that we are not at a disadvantage by having the Holy Spirit. In fact, the New Testament calls the Holy Spirit the Spirit of Jesus Christ on several occasions.[66] The same Jesus who walked the streets of Galilee and Jerusalem 2000 years ago walks with you through his Spirit. You are not alone, you are not abandoned, and you are not powerless. You have direct access to Jesus' "*incomparably great power*" (Ephesians 1:19a).

---

64 John 16:7, John 6:60, Mark 9:32, Luke 18:34.

65 John 2:22, 12:16, 14:12.

66 Philippians 1:19, Acts 16:7, Galatians 4:6, Romans 8:9. He is also called the Spirit of the Father in Matthew 10:20 and John 15:26.

My grandfather once said, "Jesus does not want warriors, he wants witnesses" (see Acts 1:8). In many ways this thought sums up this 21-day journey. We can only truly lead others to Jesus when we have first been with Jesus.

It is a simple but important truth that Jesus is the one who empowers our witness for him (1 Corinthians 3:6-7). When we walk with Jesus we take him with us whenever we witness to someone. Maybe we need to focus less on perfecting the arguments for conversion to Christianity and more on getting our walk with God healthy. When our walk with God is healthy, Jesus can walk others to himself through us!

Application

Scripture: *"We are therefore Christ's ambassadors, as though God were making his appeal through us."* 2 Corinthians 5:20

Key thought: "The Great Commission is not an option to be considered, it is a command to be obeyed"—Hudson Taylor.

Action: Don't go it alone. First, go to your local Church and talk to other believers about how you can go out into your community to witness and make disciples together. Then go!

DAY 19

Walking with Jesus through the Church

The heart of the Church

Jesus said, "*I will build my church, and the gates of Hades will not overcome it*" (Matthew 16:18). The Greek word that the English Bible translates as Church is *ekklésia* and it simply means "gathering" or "assembly." The Church is a gathering of people who have heard God's call to come out of the world's way of living to begin living together for the Kingdom of Heaven on Earth.

The Bible gives much instruction for how Churches should operate and behave. Character traits like kindness, gentleness, and self-control are upheld as essential things that a Church should embody.[67] In the midst of the New Testament's many teachings on the Church, the Apostles Paul and John both elevate one idea and place it at the heart of a healthy Church, and this idea is love.[68]

---

[67] Galatians 5:22-23, Ephesians 6:10-18, 2 Peter 1:5-9.
[68] 1 Corinthians 13:13, 1 John 5:2, 2 John 1:6.

Jesus himself says that the greatest commandment in the Old Testament is to love God and the second greatest is to love others (Matthew 22:36-40). It is interesting that when Jesus looks forward to the Church age, and not back to the time of the law, he says, "*A new command I give you: Love one another. As I have loved you, so you must love one another*" (John 13:34). Jesus reduces the two commands of the law to one command, and just in case anyone thinks this is an isolated comment, Jesus quickly repeats this stating, "*My command is this: Love each other as I have loved you*" (John 15:12). Jesus then tells us that we should lay down our lives for our friends and repeats his command a third time, saying, "*This is my command: Love each other*" (John 15:12-17).

What are we to make of this? Is Jesus saying we no longer need to love God, and we only need to love others? No. Jesus is saying that we love God through loving others. The Apostle Paul tells us this when he says, "*For the entire law is fulfilled in keeping this one command: 'Love your neighbor as yourself'*" (Galatians 5:14).[69] What this means is that the Church is a place where we love God by loving others.[70]

Acts 2:42 tells us how the very first Church did this, saying: "*They devoted themselves to the apostles' teaching and to fellowship, to the breaking of bread and to prayer*" (Acts 2:42). Today we will look at these four things, under the headings of: the Word of God, fellowship, community, and prayer.

The Word of God in the Church

At the start of the book of Acts we see an interesting transition take place. Jesus ascends to Heaven and the Apostles need to learn to manage the Church without his direct instructions. Immediately, we see the Apostle

[69] See also, 1 John 4:7-5:3, specifically 1 John 4:7, 11, 21.
[70] Mark 9:41, 1 John 3:16.

Peter turn to the Bible (Acts 1:20). In doing this, Peter shows us that if we seek to know God's will, we should turn to his Word.

At the heart of any healthy Church is a love for the Word of God and a love for training people in the Word of God. We see this focus in Paul's instruction to Timothy that "*All Scripture is God-breathed and is useful for teaching, rebuking, correcting and training in righteousness*" (2 Timothy 3:16). If we seek to walk others to God, we must walk them to his Word. For this to happen, we must be learning the Word and learning how to walk with God through his Word. The Apostle John said, "*If anyone obeys his word, love for God is truly made complete in them*" (1 John 2:5a). This verse gives us a clear pathway towards making mature disciples in our Churches, and this is simply teaching people to obey the Bible.

The Bible is the voice of God to the Church. When we read the Bible we know we are reading the very words of God. And when we teach others to obey the Bible we know we are leading them faithfully.

Church fellowship

The British preacher Charles Spurgeon once met with a congregation member who had decided to keep his Christian faith but leave the local Church. There was a coal fire in the room where the two men were meeting, and as the man told his pastor he was going to leave the Church to practice his faith privately, Spurgeon quietly took a single coal out of the fire and put it on the floor in the middle of the two men. They both sat there quietly as the lone coal slowly lost its heat and went dark. Just before it went out completely, Spurgeon picked it back up and put it in the fire with the other coals. It immediately came alight again. The man said to Spurgeon, "I understand".

This simple story illustrates the necessity of being in Christian community. Like many other people, I have sat through Church meetings where horrible sins that leaders had committed had to be discussed and dealt with. Moments like this can either turn us away from Jesus or turn us to Jesus. The truth is that these situations have been a part of Church life since the very beginning of the Church. In 1 Corinthians 5:1-2 we see the Apostle Paul reprimanding sexual sin in the local Church, and there are numerous examples of people seeking to use the Church for their own financial gain recorded in the Bible. Thankfully, the Church went on to become an unmatched force for good in the world due to the dedication of its faithful followers.

Hebrews 10:25 says to "*not neglect our meeting together, as some people do, but encourage one another*" (NLT). This verse reminds us that growing in our knowledge of God, using our gifts to serve God, and helping the vulnerable in the community are all things that are difficult to do in isolation. Friend, we shouldn't allow hypocrisy from Church leaders and social issues among the congregation to stop us from being an active part of the Church community. If you have been hurt by the Church, you need to know that God and God's people have compassion and sympathy for you. Maybe a time of healing is needed where you worship with another group of believers for a season. This is a reasonable response to being hurt, but don't let the sinful actions of others rob you from living out your God given calling (Romans 11:29).

Church community

Acts 2:42 distinguishes between general fellowship and more intimate community. The words "*breaking of bread*" signify people sharing a meal together in each other's homes. This is where we get our modern-day concept of life groups from. Once a Church has over 100 people we can easily get "lost in the crowd." Being in smaller more intimate relationship with other Christians provides support and love to our lives. It is interesting that this also mirrors Jesus' own ministry, where he had an inner group of three: Peter, James and John, then the twelve disciples, and then still hundreds of disciples. Acts 2:42 teaches us that being in consistent, close community with other believers is essential for the Christian walk.

Prayer and the Church

True prayer does not originate with the mouth, it comes from the overflow of a life entirely yielded to God. Just like the power of a batter to hit a ball doesn't come from his wrists, but rather his entire body swinging as one, the prayer which moves mountains comes from the whole life being committed to God.

As we read through the Gospels, we see the central role that prayer takes in the life and ministry of Jesus. The book of Acts and the New Testament letters show us that the Apostles adopted Jesus' focus on prayer. Throughout Church history, whenever Christians sought revival, they instinctively knew to go to prayer. This teaches us that prayer is the engine of the Church (Philippians 4:6). When the Church is fervently praying it is growing, and when it is not fervently praying it is contracting (James 5:16).

Much of God's dealings with us in the Christian walk are centred around getting us to cease depending upon ourselves and to begin calling on him in prayer, so that he can heal and help us (Psalm 81:11-14). The first thing God seeks to conquer is our sin and self, but the second thing he seeks to conquer is our self-capacity to build his Church. God wants us to depend on him for holiness and harvest. When we call on him to act in prayer, we prevail against the Church's many foes (Ephesians 6:12).

In the Church and Christian walk we show our love for God by obedience to his Word and through obtaining what we need from God through prayer.

A new day

As we read on day seventeen, Hudson Taylor said, "God does not do His great works by large committees. He trains somebody to be quiet enough, and little enough and then He uses him." If your Church is struggling today, I pray you find encouragement from Hudson Taylor's words. God just needs one person to be given over to his love, his Word, fellowship, community, and prayer to turn even the toughest situation around. Today determine to be a disciple who shares God's love with others through the ideas given to us in Acts 2:42. As you do this God will bring others for you to disciple into these same truths.

Application

Scripture: *"I am writing you these things [...] so that you will know how each one must conduct himself in God's household, which is the church of the living God, the pillar and foundation of the truth."* 1 Timothy 3:14b-15, BSB

Key thought: God builds his Church through us.

Action: Church life can get so busy, analyse your priorities with those discussed today. Are there areas where changes need to be made to recenter your Church on Christ's love, the Word, fellowship, community, or prayer?

DAY 20

Walking to leave a Gospel legacy

Today we will discover how to live a life that leaves a Gospel legacy. From the outset we must ensure that our motivation in doing this is not our own glory, but to glorify God through bearing much fruit for him (John 15:8). As the Prophet Isaiah says, "*your name and renown are the desire of our hearts*" (Isaiah 26:8).

A Gospel legacy explained

Proverbs 13:22a says, *"Good people leave an inheritance to their grandchildren"* (NLT). I wonder if we have ever considered what kind of inheritance we are leaving for our family? Money is a very real thing in our society and good stewardship of resources can bless many, but it is the Gospel and spiritual things that will last (Matthew 6:19).

Hudson Taylor left one of the greatest spiritual legacies in the history of the Christian Church; the 100-300 million believers in China today are often attributed to his trust in the faithfulness of God. While the other missionaries remained largely in the safety of the capital cities, Hudson sent missionaries (often single women) into the rural inland areas of China, spreading the Gospel across the nation.

Hudson famously summarised his mission strategy by saying, "God's work done in God's way will never lack God's supply." This quote from Hudson Taylor is the result of him testing the promises of God and proving them faithful. The quote has three basic parts to it, which will help us learn how to leave a Gospel legacy.

God's work

Hudson Taylor's quote begins by clarifying that only God's work will attract God's blessing, and God's work is the Gospel. In 1 Corinthians 15:3-4, Paul summarises the basic Gospel message: *"Christ died for our sins, just as the Scriptures said. He was buried, and he was raised from the dead on the third day, just as the Scriptures said."* (NLT). About this C. S. Lewis famously wrote:

> "We are told that Christ was killed for us, that His death has washed out our sins, and that by dying He disabled death itself. That is the formula. That is Christianity. That is what has to be believed."[71]

The Gospel is God's message and if we are to see God's blessing in our lives we must make God's message our message.

In Matthew 24:14 Jesus calls the Gospel, the "*gospel of the kingdom.*" This verse highlights we are to build the Kingdom of God through our Churches. The Christian Church is always at its best when we unify to build the Kingdom of God in our communities (John 17:21). In short, the basic aspects of what it means to do God's work are: believing the

[71] C. S. Lewis. *Mere Christianity*, 55.

core Gospel message of the death and resurrection of Jesus, building the Kingdom of God through our local Churches, and loving one another.

Done God's way

God's way is to change people into the image of his Son through his love as displayed on the Cross. We learnt on day thirteen from John 3:14-15 and Charles Spurgeon that when this message is preached, people look at it and this looking enables belief. Through belief, repentance and confession arise and sin is seen and forsaken. God's love is then known and walked in through a daily habit of reading the Word and prayer. The Bible then tells us that we know with certainty we are abiding in God's love when we have been changed (1 John 2:3-5). This is God's way, but so often it is replaced with trying harder to be holy (called moralism), or other variations which Paul called *different gospels* or *no gospel at all* (Galatians 1:6-7).

It should be added here that the Bible simply calls God's way of changing us walking by the Spirit, and that as we do this God's heart for the most destitute and vulnerable in society will become dear to us (Galatians 2:10).

Will never lack God's supply

So far today we have discovered that God's work is to know and show the Gospel in local Churches so that the Kingdom of God can be built. This work is not fuelled by human strength but by God's mighty redemptive love, which is known as we walk with Jesus. When we walk in God's love through cherishing his Word, engaging in prayer, and sharing his Gospel message, the Bible assures us that we will never lack God's supply. This "supply" is twofold and can be summarised as reason and resource.

Some Christians lack a reason for their ministry to exist— meaning they need God to breathe fresh life into their organisation to bring avenues for them to share the Gospel. Other Christians have active ministries but lack financial and physical resources.

In these situations sometimes God asks us to wait on his timing and this is a very real thing, but we should wait responsibly, using this time to perform a health-check on our lives to see if we have accidentally drifted out of either God's work or God's way. We should be mature in our assessment of our lives and ministries. Jesus commanded us to make disciples in his name (Matthew 28:19). This is a clear command and it means that our goal is a continual flow of real people being developed as disciples. Churches growing through people changing Churches is not the same as a continual flow of real people being developed as disciples. We must also be watchful that human motives have not overtaken God's work and way. Human agendas and human effort can very subtly slip into our hearts, and these can be hard to detect. It is not unreasonable in this situation to perform a biblical fast and have a season focused on the core act of love at the Cross (Matthew 16:17-18). Use this time to ask God to speak and show if any sinfulness or self-agenda has crept in. Remember that God's promise of blessing is available to all people, but it is conditional on us doing his work, his way.

The Holy Spirit of power

When Hudson Taylor talks about "God's supply" he is ultimately talking about the work of the Holy Spirit. God's work is the Spirit's work, God's way is to work by his Spirit, and God's supply comes from the Holy Spirit (Zechariah 4:6).

Paul says, "*For the Spirit God gave us does not make us timid, but gives us power, love and self-discipline*" (2 Timothy 1:7). It is the Holy Spirit who enables our Christian walk and who grows our Churches.[72] All three of the

[72] 1 Peter 1:12, 1 Thessalonians 1:5, 2:13.

points discussed today are made possible as we call on the Holy Spirit to accomplish God's will in us.[73]

The Bible says that God gives his Holy Spirit to those who obey him (Acts 5:32). In his letter to the Romans, Paul begins and ends with the idea that this much-needed obedience is made possible by faith in Jesus.[74] Where the law in the Old Testament could not change our hearts, in the New Testament, the Holy Spirit pours God's love into our hearts as we walk with Jesus by faith (Romans 5:5). The Spirit can soften and make malleable even the most hardened heart.

Today, let's consider the value of possessing hearts that are full of God's love through the Holy Spirit, and then realise the benefit this brings to the next generation as they are brought up in such an environment.

We opened today with Proverbs 13:22a which says, *"Good people leave an inheritance to their grandchildren."* Living in obedience to God's command to rely on Jesus to change us and make us fruitful is the best thing we can do for future generations.[75] A legacy of worldly wealth is nothing compared to a legacy of hearts softened by God's love and therefore filled with God's Spirit.

As we live this way God is glorified by the fruit he brings from our lives, and our lives gain eternal meaning through finding our place in his redemptive plan (John 15:8). As Catherine Booth, co-founder of The Salvation Army once said, "You are not here in the world for yourself. You have been sent here for others. The world is waiting for you!"

---

[73] 1 Peter 1:2, Philippians 2:13.

[74] Romans 1:5, 16:26, NIV, BSB.

[75] Hebrews 8:10, 10:15-16.

Application

Scripture: *"I thank God, whom I serve, as my ancestors did [...] I am reminded of your sincere faith, which first lived in your grandmother Lois and in your mother Eunice and, I am persuaded, now lives in you also."* 2 Timothy 1:3-5

Key thought: The greatest thing we can do for our families and friends is lead them to Jesus.

Action: Think through how you can centre your life and family in the mission of God in a greater way. Spend time considering how your decisions today will impact your family in the decades to come. Consider writing a mission statement for your life, including the key things you want to be remembered for.

DAY 21

Walking others into eternity

This 21-day journey opened with God's command and promise to Abraham in Genesis 17:1-2. Today we will finish this journey by looking at the eternal rewards that come from walking with Jesus.

Jesus' eternal message

In Jesus' Sermon on the Mount, he says, "*Do not store up for yourselves treasures on earth, where moths and vermin destroy, and where thieves break in and steal. But store up for yourselves treasures in heaven, where moths and vermin do not destroy, and where thieves do not break in and steal*" (Matthew 6:19-20).

This statement from Jesus points us away from living for this life and towards living for eternity. Jesus tells us here and in so many other places to invest our time, resources, and lives in storing up an inheritance in Heaven. If Jesus was preaching in our modern world, I imagine he might say to us: "Don't build multiple investment properties for yourself on Earth or live to accumulate large share portfolios. But invest in heavenly homes and accumulate a large share portfolio in Heaven by inviting others to share in Heaven."

Jesus is encouraging us to take up a purpose and cause in this life that rewards us eternally. The Gospel is an invitation to live for something far better than anything the world can offer (John 3:16).

Jesus' eternal challenge

Perhaps the most uncomfortable aspect of living for eternity is that it involves dying to the things of this world. A few days before his crucifixion Jesus likens a person who lives for eternity to a kernel of wheat that must first die to then produce plentiful new growth (John 12:24). Jesus explains this by saying, "*Anyone who loves their life will lose it, while anyone who hates their life in this world will keep it for eternal life*" (John 12:25).

The Apostle Paul summaries this powerful truth when he says, "*For if we have been united with him in a death like his, we will certainly also be united with him in a resurrection like his*" (Romans 6:5). It would be a wise person who spent time meditating on the words "*if*" and "*certainly*" in this powerful verse.

To live for eternity on Earth we need God's power and this power only comes to those who have died to the world. I opened this book with the admission that I once realised I was educated far beyond my level of repentance. Friend, the Church does not need more people who are educated but disobedient to the ways of God and therefore powerless. We must remember that true knowledge of the Word of God is found not in "degrees", but in the degree to which we are co-crucified with Jesus.[76] This truth more than any other shows us the nature of God's eternal Kingdom, that is, God's Kingdom is not focused on our comfort, but rather on us being like

[76] Galatians 2:20, 2 Timothy 2:20-21.

Christ. And we know we are like Christ when we learn to serve and sacrifice in the same way Jesus did at the Cross (1 John 2:6). As the missionary Jim Elliot said, "He is no fool who gives what he cannot keep, to gain what he cannot lose."

If you can feel the Spirit of God pulling at your heart and directing you to leave the things of this world to live for eternal things, then know that you are not alone.

Living for eternity

In the early 2000s it was common to hear pastors in Sydney talk about "Mr Eternity." Mr Eternity was the name given to a former homeless man named Arthur Stace. Arthur was powerfully converted to Jesus at an inner-city Church and then spent the rest of his life writing the word "Eternity" on the footpaths of Sydney with chalk. After his death in the 1960s, Christians kept Arthur's legacy alive by continuing to write "eternity" on the ground. This story took a dramatic turn in the year 2000 at the New Year's Eve fireworks. As the millennium took place the world turned its eyes to the iconic Sydney Harbour fireworks display. It is estimated that over a billion people watched as the word "Eternity" appeared in the middle of the Sydney Harbour Bridge in Arthur's memorable handwriting. This humble man walked the streets of Sydney writing the word eternity on the ground in donated chalk, and God took this simple gesture and broadcast it around the globe.

In John 12:49-50 Jesus tells us that the Father sent him to lead us into eternal life. The reason why Jesus makes such a passionate plea for us to accept his offer of eternal life is because he knows what happens when we say no. Friend, I realise this isn't popular nowadays, but the Bible says in Matthew 25:46 that if we don't say yes to "*eternal life*" we will endure "*eternal punishment*" (This is because God is just and he cannot leave wrongdoing unpunished). Once we realise there are two eternities, we find great motivation to live our lives sharing the Gospel with others.

Jesus says that Satan is the ruler of this world (John 14:30). When we register this truth and look at Jesus' language in the Gospels we come to realise that the Father sent his Son to rescue us. We are like hostages being held captive by a hostile army and Jesus is the Saviour sent in to rescue us (2 Timothy 2:26). I imagine that if you are reading this in even a semi-affluent area on a sunny day this might be a hard truth to take in. If this is the case then Jesus invites us to look closer at the reality of our world and the lives of those around us.

If you are in an affluent area then notice your neighbours enduring long days at work to pay off their mortgages. Look closely and see the loneliness in the homes all around you and the despair driving people to addiction. Hardship and hopelessness are not reserved only for those in third-world countries, they are all around us and evidence of the spiritual reality that the Bible points to (John 12:46). People like Arthur Stace came to understand this and spent their lives presenting the hope of eternal life, which Jesus called the Kingdom of God and paradise.

Today God is inviting you to live your life for something far greater than any worldly cause, which is to invite others into eternal life through following Jesus. In the same way that we can live for an upcoming holiday, we are invited to live for the upcoming eternal Kingdom of God (Colossians 3:2).

A long walk with Jesus

While being questioned by the religious leaders Jesus said to them, "*My kingdom is not of this world [...] But now my kingdom is from another place*" (John 18:36). Through an act of faith, we are called to live our lives in this world for the next world. To adopt Jesus' language, we are called to live our lives in this world for the reward that will come to us in "*another place.*"

To illustrate this, I want to ask you to finish this 21-day journey by going outside tonight and looking up at the star Arcturus.[77] As you look at this mighty star, take note that the light from Arcturus you are looking at has taken 37 years to reach Earth. This means the light you see began in a distant star 37 years ago and is ending its life by crashing into your eyes. By looking at this star and catching its light you are literally touching something "*not of this world*"; something "*from another place*" (John 18:36).

Just as light from Arcturus has been travelling to Earth for the past 37 years, light from Arcturus will be travelling to Earth for the next 37 years. Friend, determine today that in 37 years' time you (or your descendants on your behalf) will meet the light Arcturus released today without regret, having walked with Jesus and having walked others to Jesus.

Allow the habit that you have formed of reading the Word and being with Jesus over the past 21 days to continue. Start by reading through the Gospel of Luke and calling on God in prayer. Determine that you will walk with God all the days of your life.

An eternal purpose

As this 21-day journey ends, we must decide what we are going to live for in this life. We can live for many things in this world, but Jesus implores us to look up and see both the brevity of this life and the eternal nature of the next life. The Bible says our life is "*a mist that appears for a little while and then vanishes*" (James 4:14). To illustrate this, a pastor I knew lit a match while preaching on this verse and pointed the congregation to the puff of smoke that came off the end of the matchstick. This tiny puff of smoke represents our life next to eternity. When we live for the things of this world, we are living for things that are "*here today and gone tomorrow*"

[77] Arcturus straddles the equator so it is often visible to most of the world, but if this is not the case for you any star will do.

(Matthew 6:30, GNT). Through the Gospel, God is inviting us to live for eternal things, and the way we do this is by spending our days inviting others into eternity on behalf of Jesus (2 Corinthians 5:20).

Death is not the end

The Bible says that in eternity "*He will wipe every tear from their eyes. There will be no more death' or mourning or crying or pain, for the old order of things has passed away*" (Revelation 21:4). No matter what this life brings, take heart that in the Eternal City we will be restored, and the struggle to live for God and build his Church will finally be over. The Early Church theologian Augustine describes this saying:

> "Who does not long for that city, where no friend leaves and no enemy enters, where no one tries or disturbs us, no one divides the people of God, no one wearies God's Church?... We will have God as our common sight, we will have God as our common possession, we will have God as our common peace."[78]

The Apostle Peter wrote that through Jesus' death and resurrection we are offered an "*entrance*" into these eternal things (2 Peter 1:11). Those who walk with Jesus reach behind the curtain of creation and touch eternity. And those who walk others to Jesus help kindle eternal life and light in people's lives.

The truth is that there is no higher thing to live for or greater cause to take up than being an ambassador of God's eternal love. People have searched the world and never found anything greater than God's invitation to walk before him and walk others to him.

---

[78] Enarrations in Psalms, 84.10. Cited in Daley, *The Hope of the Early Church.* Page 147.

Application

Scripture: *"For God so loved the world that he gave his one and only Son, that whoever believes in him shall not perish but have eternal life"* John 3:16. Also, read 2 Peter 1:3-11.

Key thought: The Kingdom of God is real.

Action: Take time to comprehend that God wants to use your life for an eternal purpose! Write down three things you can do differently to redirect your life towards God's eternal purpose. Determine that you will continue to walk with God, as you have for the past 21 days.

LIFE GROUP INFORMATION

Walking with Jesus includes being in community with other believers. To assist with this, Life Group discussion questions are included. The table below outlines how the Life Group discussion questions are intended to be used in relation to the 21-day journey, assuming a Wednesday meeting.

Monday	Tuesday	Wednesday	Thursday	Friday	Saturday	Sunday
		Life Group One				
Day 1	Day 2	Day 3. Life Group Two.	Day 4	Day 5	Day 6	Day 7
Day 8	Day 9	Day 10. Life Group Three.	Day 11	Day 12	Day 13	Day 14
Day 15	Day 16	Day 17. Life Group Four.	Day 18	Day 19	Day 20	Day 21
		Life Group Five				

The Life Group discussion questions, along with the 21-day journey, take people through a pathway covering the themes outlined in the table below.

Sermon	Focus	Outcome	The Way He Walked
Week 1	Invitation	Understanding that God invites us to walk with him, through following Jesus	Day 1
Week 2	Relationship	Learning the Christian walk is relational in nature, not religious or institutional	Days 2-7
Week 3	Transformation	Letting go of the past, to walk in new life	Days 8-12
Week 4	Formation	Growing strong through key habits of faith	Days 13-17
Week 5	Mission	Beginning to lead others to Christ	Days 18-21
Week 6 (Optional)	Legacy	Our faith can impact the next generation	Days 20-21

See Church Series Information section for more.

Life Group discussion questions

Week one: God invites us to walk with him

Focus: Invitation

Main Scripture: "'*Come, follow me', Jesus said, 'and I will send you out to fish for people.*'" (Matthew 4:19)

- Discuss what it means to walk before God by following Jesus. Pay attention to the words "follow" and "Jesus."
- Read Luke 5:1-11 and discuss the four "simple points" from the Bible story detailed on day one of the 21-day journey. See section, "How this book works."
- Identify what you are following at this point in your life, for instance, a culture, a career path, or a sporting team. How do these things contribute to or compete with you walking before God?
- Before this 21-day journey begins, spend some time discussing what it may look like to cease following some things in order to follow Jesus wholeheartedly.
- What does it mean to partner with God to see change accomplished in your life? What role do the Bible, prayer, and Christian community play in changing us?
- Read 1 John 2:6 and discuss what it means to live like Jesus did.
- Share a time with each other where God has changed you or something you wish to see changed in your life.
- Pray about these things together.

Week two: God seeks a relationship with us

Focus: Relationship
Main Scripture: "*When Abram was ninety-nine years old, the Lord appeared to him and said, 'I am God Almighty; walk before me faithfully and be blameless. Then I will make my covenant between me and you and will greatly increase your numbers.*'" (Genesis 17:1-2, ESV)

- Begin by discussing what it means to accept God's invitation to walk with him.
- What does it mean to be changed by walking in God's love? (2 John 6).
- Discuss how the Apostle John tells us to "*walk in love*" and how this corresponds to the Apostle Paul telling us to "*walk in the Spirit*" (2 John 6, Galatians 5:25, NKJV).
- What does it mean to be rooted and established in love? (Ephesians 3:15-17).
- How will your life be different when you allow God's love to change you, as opposed to being "condemned" into change? (John 3:16-17)
- Based on the material on days five to seven, discuss how for something to be resurrected, it must first be dead (John 12:24). How does the core Christian message of being crucified with Christ, so that we can then rise with Christ, sit with you? (Romans 6:5-8, Galatians 2:20)
- How will your family and friends be impacted as you represent Jesus' love and sacrificial glory to them daily?

Week three: Walking free from our past and pain

Focus: Transformation
Main Scripture: "*So they pulled their boats up on shore, left everything and followed him.*" (Luke 5:11)

- Like us, Peter had to trust Jesus for his real-life needs. Consider that Peter had to trust Jesus for a new income, social group, and purpose when he walked away from his trade and fishing community. Do you think it was easy or hard for Peter to do this? (Luke 5:1-11).
- In Luke 5:8, Peter remarks to Jesus that he is a "*sinful man.*" Peter had to walk away from his sinful lifestyle to follow Jesus. Days eight to ten discussed three areas related to sin that we need to walk away from: partial obedience, a low view of holiness, and comparing ourselves to others instead of Jesus' love for us. Pause in your group to pray and ask God to show you which of these areas you need to walk away from.
- Share with each other what God is prompting you on.
- Days eleven and twelve discuss how God uses suffering for an eternal purpose in our lives. Discuss how this scriptural truth can help you walk <u>through</u> earthly pain into a new eternal purpose.
- Noting the material under the heading "Learning to call on God" on day seven, end your group time by calling on God to help change you in the areas you feel need walking away from (Psalm 50:15).

Week four. Walking with Jesus

Focus: Formation
Main Scripture: "*Look to Me, and be saved, All you ends of the earth.*" (Isaiah 45:22, NKJV)

The third section of the book is dedicated to getting the basic areas of our Christian life working, so that God can then do fruitful and fantastic things through us.

- What do you think the relationship is between us bearing fruit and our spiritual "health"? (John 15:1-12)
- Day fourteen connects the dots between looking, believing, and our actions through a simple story about a "flannelgraph" board. Discuss how what we look at determines our mindset and then our actions.
- Read the Scripture medley of Numbers 21:9 and John 3:14-15 on day thirteen. Discuss how looking at God's love for us on the Cross is the genesis (beginning) of believing.
- Day fifteen discusses that repentance involves leaving sin (Acts 3:19) and coming to the Kingdom of God (Mark 1:15). Why is it important to leave sin by coming to the Kingdom? (See section "Repentance as it should be" on day fifteen.)
- On day sixteen the quote from Donald Bloesch says: "The righteousness of God is not a prize that can be earned by works of love but a gift that enables man to do such works." How does this thought change your understanding of the Christian life? (Romans 1:17)
- Why is it important to move forward in our life with God through seeking to reach others with the Gospel? How does doing this grow

our own faith? (See section "Having faith for others deepens our faith" on day sixteen.)

- We often get confused about what our unique calling is. Consider that our calling can simply be what we are naturally passionate about combined with God's missional purpose. What are you passionate about and how can you use this for God's glory in a greater way?
- Do you feel God calling you to take a step of faith in some area of your life? If yes, pray together about this and take steps to say yes to God.

Week five: Walking others to Jesus

Focus: Mission
Main Scripture: "*God was reconciling the world to himself in Christ, not counting people's sins against them. And he has committed to us the message of reconciliation. We are therefore Christ's ambassadors, as though God were making his appeal through us.*" (2 Corinthians 5:19-20a)

- Read the story of Andrew bringing his brother Simon/Peter to Jesus, what can we learn from this story? (John 1:40-42).
- What role do you think the idea of storing up "*treasures*" in Heaven and our life being a "*vapour*" played in Andrew bringing his brother Peter to Jesus? (Matthew 6:19, James 4:14).
- The missionary Hudson Taylor said, "The Great Commission is not an option to be considered, it is a command to obey." How does this comment sit with you?
- How should the four points of the Great Commission change our daily priorities? (see day eighteen)
- Discuss the story of Arthur Stace on day twenty-one. Google the image of the word eternity on the Sydney Harbour Bridge in the year 2000 and discuss how God was able to do something great with such a humble gesture.
- Name one person in your world that you can reach out to tomorrow to touch with the love of Jesus in some way, big or small.
- Spend time in prayer together and ask God to do two things. First, give you the courage and conviction to reach out to the person you named. Second, to open this person's heart to be ready to hear the Gospel through you.

Optional sixth Life Group. Leaving a Gospel Legacy

Focus: Legacy
Main Scripture: *"Good people leave an inheritance to their grandchildren."* (Proverbs 13:22a)

- Read the description in the first two paragraphs on day twenty and discuss what it means to leave a Gospel legacy.
- What does it mean to live for God's glory as outlined on day three? Note that God's glory is hallmarked by sacrifice (Mark 10:45).
- Consider your children or grandchildren (if you don't have them, imagine them), and think about the legacy you are leaving for them. What would their lives look like in the future if you kept walking with Jesus for the rest of your life in the same way you have over the past 21 days?
- What changes to your daily schedule need to be made to make this continual walking with God possible?
- Choose a book of the Bible that you, as a group, can read through systematically over the next few months to help you keep walking with Jesus.
- Consider 2 Corinthians 5:7 and what it means to walk forward in your life and ministry based on faith and not sight.
- Remember that it is our work to abide and God's work to grow. Discuss this considering the following scriptural phrases: "I will build my Church", "the Lord added", "God made it grow" (Matthew 16:18, Acts 2:47, 1 Corinthians 3:6).
- End by praying together about three things. First, what God is calling you to do for his glory. Second, any changes you need to make

to your schedule to enable this to happen. Third, for God's power to work through you.

End by watching the following video.

Billy Graham, "Billy Graham's 99th Birthday: Notable Reflections."
Billy Graham Evangelistic Association
https://www.youtube.com/watch?v=pz4pFVVMzLw

CHURCH SERIES INFORMATION

The Church wide series builds on the four "simple points" outlined on "day one" to take people on a five-week pathway from invitation to mission, with an optional sixth week on the topic of legacy:

Sermon	Focus	Outcome	The Way He Walked
Week 1	Invitation	Understanding that God invites us to walk with him, through following Jesus	Day 1
Week 2	Relationship	Learning the Christian walk is relational in nature, not religious or institutional	Days 2-7
Week 3	Transformation	Letting go of the past, to walk in new life	Days 8-12
Week 4	Formation	Growing strong through key habits of faith	Days 13-17
Week 5	Mission	Beginning to lead others to Christ	Days 18-21
Week 6 (Optional)	Legacy	Our faith can impact the next generation	Days 20-21

The table below outlines how the Church wide series operates in relation to the 21-day journey (the Life Group outlines are included after the daily readings for ease of use):

Monday	Tuesday	Wednesday	Thursday	Friday	Saturday	Sunday
						Sermon one. Introduction.
		Life Group One. Introduction.				Sermon Two
Day 1	Day 2	Day 3. Life Group Two.	Day 4	Day 5	Day 6	Sermon Three. Day 7
Day 8	Day 9	Day 10. Life Group Three.	Day 11	Day 12	Day 13	Sermon Four. Day 14
Day 15	Day 16	Day 17. Life Group Four.	Day 18	Day 19	Day 20	Sermon Five. Day 21
		Life Group Five				

An optional sixth sermon outline and Life Group discussion questions are included, covering the theme of legacy; specifically, how our faith can impact the next generations. This is based on days 20-21 in the 21-day journey.

Sermon outlines are included at the end of the book.

Note: sermons 1-3 are forward-looking in nature, covering material the participants are yet to read. Sermons 4-5 are a review, covering material the participants have already read. It is good to be mindful of this when delivering the message to the congregation.

Summary of the book for Church leaders

The Way He Walked takes people through a 21-day journey on how to walk with Jesus and then walk others to Jesus. The book has four sections which come from Jesus' invitation to Peter in Luke 5 to follow him. These are:

1. God's invitation to walk with him
2. Walking free from our past and pain
3. Walking as Jesus walked
4. Walking others to Jesus

Writing style

The book follows Jesus' teaching method and uses allegory (story) to translate theological truth into common language and therefore people's everyday lives. Each reading is relatively short, about 10 minutes of easy reading, with the intention that this allows time for prayer and reflection. Each day's reading contains an application.

The book is intentionally concise so that it can be effectively used by busy people in the modern world.

Contents summary

The book seeks to move people from a general understanding of who Jesus is and into a living relationship with him. Achieving this goal begins in section one through introducing the reader to the Father's love on day two, then the life of Jesus on day three, and the ministry of the Holy Spirit on day four. These initial three days serve as a "meet and greet" between the reader and God. The next two days cover the Gospel, specifically the invitation to "die to self" and "rise to new life." These two days firstly seek to show the reader that God offers to put to death addictions that are plaguing them or past hurts that are consuming them (John 12:24). It is only through God's divine power that these things can truly be made "dead" in us and our lives freed from them (Galatians 2:20). Secondly, day six presents God's offer of resurrection life. Day seven operates as a bridge between sections one and two and discusses Jesus' invitation to live a purposeful life.

Section two invites the reader to walk away from their past through moving away from three key things: partial obedience, comparison to the world and others, and a low view of holiness. After a day on each of these topics, two days are then spent talking about how hardship orientates us to eternal things, and then how to walk with "a God who allows pain."

Section three takes the reader through the basic ideas associated with following Jesus: belief, repentance, confession, faith, and God's personal call to each of us. Great care is made in this section to present the Gospel of grace and not moralism, which is all too common nowadays (Philippians 2:13, Galatians 1:6-7). The change mechanism of the Christian life is God's love, which is explained through the process of Christ living in us through his Word and Spirit abiding in us (John 15:5-10, Romans 5:5, Hebrews 8:10; 10:15-16, etc). Jesus' words to Nicodemus in John 3:14-15 (Numbers 21:9) and Charles Spurgeon's thoughts on these are used to highlight the change process of the Christian walk. This is as follows: looking at God's love on the Cross (Jesus), through this looking believing can happen, and then confession and repentance. This section is designed to help the reader "get the basics right." When we get the basics of walking with God right—belief, repentance, confession, and faith—God can then do fruitful and fantastic things through us.

Lastly, in section four the idea of walking others to Jesus is covered. This section does not outline an evangelism and discipleship "system" or "program." Rather, a day is spent on each of the following areas: the Great Commission, the local Church, leaving a Gospel legacy, and eternity. The intention here is to inspire the reader to invite others to Jesus through the local Church.

In summary, this book is for people seeking an authentic experience of faith in Jesus (Ephesians 3:19, see day four). The book isn't designed to teach abstract theological concepts about Christianity, instead, it's designed to help people personally meet the God of Christianity—Jesus.

Outline of key themes for the 21 readings

Section one

- Day 1: Introduction
- Days 2-4: Meeting God: Father, Son, and Spirit.
- Days 5-6: The Gospel. Death and resurrection.
- Day 7: This day operates as a bridge between sections, focusing on living with purpose.

Section two

- Days 8-10: These three days are dedicated to walking away from our past just like Peter did. Three modern areas of struggle are covered: obedience, comparison, and holiness.
- Day 11-12: These two days discuss how suffering points us to the eternal and walking with a God who allows hardship.

Section three

- Days 13-16: These days are dedicated to "getting the basics right" so that God can do fantastic and fruitful things in our lives. These basics are: belief, repentance, confession, and faith.
- Day 17: This day operates as a bridge between sections, talking about God's personal call to walk with him and walk others to him.

Section four

- Days 18-21: This final section takes inspiration from Andrew walking his brother Peter to Jesus. Across these four days key areas of a missional Christian life are discussed, inspiring the reader to walk others to Jesus through the local Church.

Note: The decision was made not to dedicate specific days to the Bible and prayer in this 21-day journey, instead these two primary elements of the Christian life are woven into all the readings.

Sermon outline week one—detailed

Title: God invites us to walk with him.
Main Scripture: "'*Come, follow me,' Jesus said, 'and I will send you out to fish for people.*'" (Matthew 4:19)
Sermon focus: Invitation.
Focus explanation: Jesus invites, or calls us, to follow him.

This message operates as an introduction to the idea of both walking with God by following Jesus, and the idea that God wants to change us to be like Jesus.

Part one: We are all following someone or something (10 minutes)

- Peter was following the trade and culture of a fisherman when Jesus called him to leave this and follow him (Luke 5:11).
- Identify the main things people are following, such as a culture, tradition, desire, or habit.
- Note the examples at the end of day one, and how God called these people to leave what they were following to seek after him (1 Corinthians 1:26).

Part two: Being open to following Jesus afresh and anew over the next 21 days (10 minutes)

- In preparation for the start of the 21-day journey, note that Jesus allows hardship to get our attention in order to change us (Acts 9:16).
- Note the change God seeks to make in our lives. He seeks to change us into the image of his Son and give us a new purpose in life (1 Peter 2:9).
- In preparation for the start of the 21-day journey, ask if people are open to change, specifically, changing what they are following like

Peter did. Emphasise how hard it must have been for Peter to just walk away from his livelihood.

Part three: Only God can truly change us (10 minutes)

- End the message by teaching that true change in the Christian life is achieved by God working in us (Philippians 2:13), and that God works through three key things: his Word, prayer, and Christian community.
- Encourage people to be diligent in reading the Scriptures, prayer, and Christian community (life groups) over the next 21 days, knowing that the Holy Spirit will supernaturally work through these seemingly "ordinary" means to do wonderful things in our lives.
- Close the message by sharing a time from your own life when God changed you through his Word, prayer, and the Church community. You could also use the life story from one of the Bible characters listed at the end of day one.
- Pray with the congregation, inviting God into their lives afresh and anew over the next 21 days (Romans 5:5).

Sermon outline week one—brief

Sermon focus: Invitation.

Part one:

- Peter changed what he was following; how do we do likewise?

Part two:

- God wants to change us, but we must be willing to change. In preparation for the start of the 21-day journey, encourage people to be open to change.

Part three:

- Only God can truly change us.
- End the message by teaching that true change in the Christian life is achieved by God working in us (Philippians 2:13).
- Close the message by sharing a time from your own life when God changed you.

Sermon outline week two—detailed

Title: God seeks a relationship with us.
Main Scripture: "*When Abram was ninety-nine years old, the Lord appeared to him and said, "'I am God Almighty; walk before me faithfully and be blameless. Then I will make my covenant between me and you and will greatly increase your numbers.*'" (Genesis 17:1-2, ESV).
Sermon focus: Relationship.
Focus explanation: In Christianity, God invites us into a personal relationship with himself. We are not called into a "religious system" or "institution", but rather, to walk before God (Old Testament), or follow Jesus (New Testament).

This message operates as a "meet and greet" between the people and their triune God. Introducing them to the Father's love, the Son's glory, and the Holy Spirit's ministry.

Also, note the four stages of Peter's call to follow Jesus on day one, under the heading "How this book works." This week's sermon covers stage one.

Part one: Walking before a loving Father (10 minutes)

- Retell the story from the life of the Apostle John found at the start of day two.
- God's love is the change agent of the Christian life. We need to be "*rooted and established*" in God's love for the Christian walk to work (Ephesians 3:17). We are rooted and established in God's love through the Holy Spirit, when we live consistently in God's Word. (Romans 5:5, John 15:7).
- Encourage people to begin their day by establishing themselves in God's love, through his Word. Contrast against other things we establish our minds in daily, such as social media, news etc.

Part two: Walking in the Son's heavenly glory. (10 minutes)

- Paint the picture of Solomon's golden throne as described on day three.
- Discuss religious glory. See day three, religious glory and source two.
- Discuss worldly glory. See day three, worldly glory and source one.
- Contrast by outlining heavenly "sacrificial" glory. See day three, God's glory and source three (Mark 10:45).
- Encourage people to walk like Jesus did, showing God's love through self-sacrifice (1 John 2:6).

Part three: Walking in the Spirit and love (10 minutes)

- Discuss how in Christian theology a key thing the Holy Spirit comes to do is fill us with God's love. An explanation of this is found on day two, where it says: "It is good to notice that when the Apostle John tells us to "*walk in love*", it corresponds to the Apostle Paul telling us to "*walk in the Spirit*" (2 John 6, Galatians 5:25, NKJV).
- Discuss how only the Holy Spirit can cause us to be filled with God's love. Read Romans 5:5 and read one of the quotes from John Owen, Tim Keller, or John Piper on day four.
- Using Romans 5:5 and the above quotes, end the sermon by pausing in stillness and prayer, asking the Holy Spirit to fill the hearts of the people with God's love—afresh and anew.

(If you have people you think are unsaved, be sure to mention the Gospel message and tell them that repentance is needed for God's love to enter their hearts).

Sermon outline week two—brief

Sermon focus: Relationship

Part one:

- We are invited to walk before God and the way we do this is through following Jesus.

Part two:

- We follow Jesus through embracing a lifestyle that is about helping and blessing others (Mark 10:45).

Part three:

- We ultimately follow Jesus and walk before God through the power of the Holy Spirit. It is God's Holy Spirit who fills us with his love and helps us live for others (Romans 5:5).

Sermon outline week three—detailed

Title: Walking free from our past and pain.
Main Scripture: "*So they pulled their boats up on shore, left everything and followed him.*" (Luke 5:11).
Sermon focus: Transformation.
Focus explanation: Peter said yes to Jesus' invitation to follow him by walking away from his past. We are called to do the same and leave all to follow Jesus.

Last week we discussed how we are invited to walk with God. This covered the first stage of Jesus' call to Peter to follow him. This week's sermon covers the second stage (see day one, under the heading "How this book works").

Part one: Walking away from our past (10 minutes)

- Peter was called to leave the trade of fishing behind, and he took immediate action to do this by grounding his boat on the shore. Peter's actions remind us that to walk effectively before Jesus we need to cease walking before other things in our lives. What areas of our lives do we need to walk away from, so that we can be free to wholly follow Jesus? You can use the three areas covered on days eight to ten to help discuss this point. That is, in what area is God calling for greater obedience, a higher view of holiness, and to swap comparison with others to viewing ourselves in light of God's love for us?

Part two: Walking away from our pain. (15 minutes)

- Present the idea that another thing that stops us from walking with God is how we view suffering.

- Day eleven told the story of Horatio Spafford. Retell this story or use one from your own life. Connect the story with the idea that God allows pain for a purpose and this purpose is getting us to refocus our lives on his eternal Kingdom and cause (2 Corinthians 4:17, see day twelve).
- Note the quote from Charles Stanley on day twelve that, "The dark moments of our life will last only so long as is necessary for God to accomplish His purpose in us." This quote teaches us that once we reach agreement with God about his purpose for our pain, the cloud can lift, moving us forward in life. What areas discussed in part one of this sermon do we need to reach agreement with God about?
    - An area where God is calling for greater obedience?
    - An area where God is calling for greater holiness?
    - An area where God is calling us to compare ourselves to his Son, and not others?

Part three: Walking into a new future. (5 minutes)

- Day seven discussed the idea that we are called to hear from God and then call on God. Spend the final moments of the sermon pausing to let people hear from God and then call on God in prayer about the thing he is prompting them about (at the end of part two of this sermon). For instance, God will speak to someone about the need to stop getting angry, and then they are to call on him in prayer, asking him to help them do this (Psalm 50:15). The idea here is to get the people talking and walking with God himself.

Sermon outline week three—brief

Sermon focus: Transformation.

Part one:

- Make the point that the first thing Peter did when he said yes to following Jesus is walk away from his past. We are to do the same (Luke 5:11).

Part two:

- Discuss how incomplete obedience needs to be walked away from to effectively walk with God (see days eight to ten).
- Discuss how God allows suffering because it draws us closer to him and his eternal purpose for our lives (2 Corinthians 4:17, see day twelve).

Part three:

- Close by encouraging people to ask God in prayer what areas are blocking them from walking with him, for example, an area of obedience, holiness, comparison, or suffering (Psalm 50:15).

Sermon outline week four—detailed

Title: Walking with Jesus.
Main Scripture: "*Look to Me, and be saved, All you ends of the earth.*" (Isaiah 45:22, NKJV).
Sermon focus: Formation.
Focus explanation: When we get the basics of the Christian walk working properly, God can do fruitful and fantastic things in our lives.

The last message covered walking away from our past, this message discusses how to walk effectively with Jesus. It does this through overviewing four fundamentals of the Christian faith: looking, believing, confessing, and repenting.

Part one: Looking, believing, and confessing (10 minutes)

- Tell the story of Charles Spurgeon's conversion found on day thirteen.
- Explain the connection between what we look at and what we think and believe (Matthew 6:22-23, see day thirteen, section "Looking and believing").
- Explain how we can look at things physically with our eyes, and then internally "look" at something in our mind by mentally dwelling on it (Matthew 6:22-23, Colossians 3:2, see day fourteen).
- Connect the dots, so to speak, between looking, believing, confessing and acting. (See flannelgraph story on day fourteen).

Part two: The Gospel moves our thinking and therefore our doing "forward" (10 minutes)

- Explain the meaning of the word repentance, which in Greek is *metanoia*: *meta* means after, and *noia* is the Greek word for mind, which makes repentance to mean "the after-mind" or "forward-understanding." (See day fifteen).

- Outline how *metanoia* (repentance) involves leaving sin and adopting a Kingdom mindset. (Acts 3:19, Mark 1:15, see day fifteen section "Repentance as it should be.")

Part three: Looking at Christ is the genesis (beginning) of believing in Christ (10 minutes)

- Present the combined Numbers 21:9 and John 3:14-15 scriptures found on day thirteen. Explain how just as the Israelites looked at the snake, we are simply to look at God's love for us, as seen through Christ on the Cross.
- Project a picture of Jesus on the Cross and stop speaking. Ask the congregation to look, silently, for a whole minute at this picture. Before you do this, read Romans 5:5 and ask the Holy Spirit to pour the love of Christ from Calvary into their hearts.

Sermon outline week four—brief

Sermon focus: Formation.

Part one:

- Explain the connection between what we look at and what we think and believe. (Matthew 6:22-23, see flannelgraph story on day fourteen).

Part two:

- Outline how *metanoia* (repentance) involves leaving sin and coming into a Kingdom mindset. (Acts 3:19, Mark 1:15, see day fifteen section "Repentance as it should be.")

Part three:

- Present the combined Numbers 21:9 and John 3:14-15 scriptures found on day thirteen. Explain how just as the Israelites looked at the snake, we are simply to look at God's love for us, as seen through Christ on the Cross.

Sermon outline week five—detailed

Title: Walking others to Jesus.
Main Scripture: "*God was reconciling the world to himself in Christ, not counting people's sins against them. And he has committed to us the message of reconciliation. We are therefore Christ's ambassadors, as though God were making his appeal through us.*" (2 Corinthians 5:19-20a).
Sermon focus: Mission.
Focus explanation: The Christian walk is only complete when we are walking others to Jesus.

Last week the message focused on getting some basic components of Christianity healthy. Now that this has been covered, this knowledge must be actualised by walking others to Jesus—as Andrew did to his brother Peter (John 1:40-42). Without this, the Christian life is a theory and not a lived reality.

Part one: Understanding the nature of our existence (10 minutes)

- Present the idea that our life is a "*vapour*" and that anything we build in this life will be lost outside of that which is done for God (Matthew 6:19).
- Contrast the above thought with God's offer of eternal life and an eternal inheritance for those who come to him (John 3:16, Hebrews 9:15).
- Explain that the Christian life is focused on producing "*fruit that will last*"; eternal fruit (John 15:16).

Part two: Understanding the call of God to reach others (10 minutes)

- Unpack the four areas of the Great Commission (Matthew 28:19-20) discussed on day eighteen.
    - We are to "go" to others, not wait for them to come to us.

  - Our missional activity should be focused on making long-term disciples of Christ.
  - Obedience to Jesus' commands is key to following him.
  - Jesus is always with us. Even when we can't see him or feel him, he will help us.

Part three: Living for eternity (10 minutes)

- Tell the story of Arthur Stace found on day twenty-one. Use it to make the point that God can multiply our small efforts to witness for him into something great (John 6:9-13).
- Talk about God's unique call to each of us, using a story from your life (or the one on day seventeen, section titled "God's call to us is rarely logical"). Ask the people what God is prompting them to do to reach others, especially things that seem illogical.
- Close by making the point that people have searched the world and never found anything greater than God's invitation to walk before him and walk others to him.

Sermon outline week five—brief

Sermon focus: Mission.

Part one:

- Present the idea that our life is a "*vapour*" and that anything we build in this life will be lost outside of that which is done for God (Matthew 6:19).

Part two:

- Unpack the four areas of the Great Commission (Matthew 28:19-20) discussed on day eighteen: going, making disciples, obeying God's commands, and that Jesus will never abandon us.

Part three:

- Talk about God's unique call to each of us, using a story from your life (or the one on day seventeen, section titled "God's call to us is rarely logical"). Ask the people what God is prompting them to do to reach others, especially things that seem illogical.

Optional sixth sermon outline—detailed

Title: Leaving a Gospel legacy.
Main Scripture: *"Good people leave an inheritance to their grandchildren."* (Proverbs 13:22a)
Sermon focus. Legacy—based on days 20-21
Focus explanation: Leaving a Gospel legacy for your children and grandchildren.

This message is designed to get people to think beyond the 21-day journey and to consider the impacts of "today's" decisions not just on themselves, but on their children and grandchildren.

Part one: A Gospel legacy begins through a sacrificial lifestyle (10 minutes)

- Note the different types of glory outlined on day three, which are: worldly glory, religious glory, or God's glory. Describe these three types of glory.
- Note that God's glory is hallmarked by sacrificing for others, which is best seen through Jesus' death at the Cross. (Mark 10:45). We are called to live like Jesus did. Focusing not on what we can get from others, but rather on what we can give to others (1 John 2:6).

Part two: Explaining a Gospel legacy (See page one on day twenty) (10 minutes)

- Explain the story of the missionary Hudson Taylor as found at the start of day twenty. Taylor focused on living for others and, in doing this, God used him to leave a great Gospel legacy.
- Ask the people what they feel their legacy would be, based on their lives so far. Try to do this in a humorous way so that it's not too "heavy."

- Encourage people to say yes to God, either in his specific call he has for them, or through continuing to walk with him each day as they have been doing over the past 21 days. Hudson Taylor's wife once said, "There hasn't been a cloud between [her] and God for many years." Can the same be said of us?

Part three: Living for the benefit of others (10 minutes)

- Ask people to think about their children and grandchildren. If they don't have them, get them to imagine their faces, or think of other children in their family or the church. Read Proverbs 13:22a, and talk about how our decision to obey and follow Jesus today will impact these future generations. 1 Timothy 1:5 gives an example of this.
- Encourage the people that a Gospel legacy is something God builds through them. Note the following scriptural phrases: "I will build my church", "the Lord added", "God made it grow" (Matthew 16:18, Acts 2:47, 1 Corinthians 3:6). Our role is to walk with Jesus and allow him to bear fruit through us (John 15:4-5).
- Close with the idea of walking by faith and not by sight (2 Corinthians 5:7). The Christian life, particularly one dedicated to building God's Kingdom and leaving a Gospel legacy, is lived by faith (and not sight) in God's plan, provision, and purpose (Proverbs 3:5-6).

Optional sixth sermon outline—brief

Sermon focus. Legacy—based on days 20-21.

Part one:

- We are called to live like Jesus did—focusing not on what we can get from others, but rather on what we can give to others. (Mark 10:45, 1 John 2:6).

Part two:

- Explain the story of the missionary Hudson Taylor as found at the start of day twenty. Ask the people what they feel their legacy would be based on their lives so far.

Part three:

- Ask people to think about their children and grandchildren, or other children in their family or the church. Read Proverbs 13:22a, and talk about how our decision to obey and follow Jesus today will impact these future generations.

BIBLIOGRAPHY

Augustine, *On The Trinity.*

Augustine, *Enarrations in Psalms.*

Bertha Spafford, *Our Jerusalem.* Doubleday, Garden City, NY, 1950.

Billy Graham, *The Holy Spirit.* Thomas Nelson, 1978.

Brian E. Daley, *The Hope of the Early Church.* Cambridge University Press, 1991.

Charles Spurgeon, *Spurgeon Sermons, Robinson Crusoe's Text, No. 1876, A Sermon Intended for Reading on Lord's-Day, December 27, 1885. Delivered by C. H. Spurgeon, At The Metropolitan Tabernacle, Newington, on August 30, 1885.* Volume 31, 1816-1876.

Charles Spurgeon, *Spurgeon Sermons, True Worship, No. 3464, A Sermon Published on Thursday, June 24, 1915, Delivered by C. H. Spurgeon at the Metropolitan Tabernacle, Newington on Thursday Evening, September, 1, 1870.* Volume 61, 3440-3495.

Charles Stanley, *30 Life Principles*. In Touch Ministries.

C. S. Lewis, *Mere Christianity.* Fontana Books, 1969.

D. L. Moody, *Secret Power, The Right Overflow.* F. H. Revell, Chicago, 1881.

Donald Bloesch, "The Sword of the Spirit: The Meaning of Inspiration", Themelios 5.3 (May 1980): 14–19.

Evelyn Christenson, *Lord Change Me.* Victor Books, 1977.

Gaebelein F. *Expository Bible Commentary, Volume Eight.* Zondervan, 1984.

Henry Frost, *Uncommon Christians.* China Inland Mission. Cornell ecommons.
https://ecommons.cornell.edu/server/api/core/bitstreams/6946f145-7489-48b6-bd15-339403fc0a9b/content

Hudson Taylor, *Hudson Taylor's Spiritual Secret.* Hendrickson Publishers, 2008.

Jerome, *The Fathers of the Church, St Jerome Commentary of Galatians.* Catholic University of America Press, 2010.

John Calvin, *Institutes of the Christian Religion.* Hendrickson Publishers, 2008.

John Owen, *The Works of John Owen, Volume 2.* Banner of Truth, 1966.

John Piper. *How to Experience the Outpouring of God's Love.* Desiring God, 2016.
www.desiringgod.org

Karl Barth, *The Christian Life, Church Dogmatics Volume IV, Part 4, Lecture Fragments.* Eerdmans, 1981.

Louie Giglio. Passion City Church, "What is Worship?"
https://www.youtube.com/watch?v=nfOxa7U8q5g

Martin Luther. *Large Catechism, Of Prayer: The Lord's Prayer.*

Michael Keller, "My Dad (Tim Keller) Listened to History to Speak the Gospel." The Gospel Coalition, 2024.
https://www.thegospelcoalition.org/article/keller-history-gospel/

Oswald Chambers, *My Utmost for His Highest.* Barbour, 1963.

Robert Mulholland, *Invitation to Journey.* Inter Varsity Press, 2016.

Ruth Paxton, *Rivers of Living Water.* Moody Publishers, 2013.

Rick Warren, *The Purpose Driven Life.* Zondervan, 2002.

Tim Keller, "Remarks from Timothy Keller & Sinclair Ferguson." Westminster Theological Seminar
https://www.youtube.com/watch?v=L7q_Aa4BJLE

Timothy Keller, *Prayer: Experiencing Awe and Intimacy with God.* Hodder and Stoughton, 2014.

Tozer, *The Radical Cross*. Moody Publishers, 2015.

Treadwell Walden, *The Great Meaning of Metanoia*. Thomas Whittaker, 1896.

www.ingramcontent.com/pod-product-compliance
Lightning Source LLC
LaVergne TN
LVHW092003080726
842905LV00026B/203
* 9 7 8 1 7 6 4 3 8 2 0 7 6 *